# Praise for *Connec*

"Philanthropists come in all shapes a.~~.~~ ~~....~~, ~~but in~~ *Connected for Good*, John Stanley describes the most common longings: for richer relationships, more gratifying acts of service, and effective giving."

**—Adam Meyerson**
President, Philanthropy Roundtable

"John, you are on to something—deeply connecting with others is an anchor element of a generous life. You have broken through with a message that our families, neighborhoods, and communities really need and a way to be generous without focusing only on the check."

**—Gordon Hartman**
Gordon Hartman Family Foundation

"John Stanley has re-imagined generosity, integrating it into the very essence of what it means to be fully alive. His insight moves us from the work of giving to the joy of connecting. And when the connection is real, the gifts that we have been given, naturally, and even effortlessly, flow to where they make a difference."

**—Monsignor Don Fischer**
Pastoral Reflections Institute

"We see it time after time—generous people digging deep to help important causes in our communities. Now, in *Connected for Good*, we learn how to move beyond just cutting the check or adding another hour of volunteer time. Generosity, as John Stanley sees it, is transformational."

**—Scott Murray**
Chairman/CEO, Murray Media

"In the world of philanthropy, we are ready for a fresh view of generosity that reconnects us to one another and brings meaning to our means."

**—Deborah Fugenschuh**

Executive Director, Donors Forum of Wisconsin

"Men and women of faith will benefit immensely from *Connected for Good*. John Stanley provides us a clear and inspiring framework for the 'why' of generosity."

**—Frank Hanna**

Author, *What Your Money Means and How to Use It Well*

"John Stanley's Generosity Gameplan has captured a masterful invitation—to what we at 1440 would call a generative giving experience, one which creates more energy than it consumes!"

**—Scott and Joanie Kriens**

Directors, 1440 Foundation

"The spirit of generosity is grounded in our sense of gratitude for all God's gifts. Appreciation then moves us to care for others. *Connected for Good* is a radical call for Catholics and all people of faith to re-create a culture of generosity for themselves, the Church, and those they care deeply about."

**—Most Reverend George Rassas**

Auxiliary Bishop of Chicago

"*Connected for Good* will challenge, inspire, and equip you to experience the true joy of generosity in all its dimensions. If you are ready to transform the way you think about your relationships, strengths, and resources, this is the book for you."

**—William E. Simon Jr.**

William E. Simon Foundation

"Despite our blessings, many of us struggle to give and receive from a place of abundance and unconditional love. Thank you, John, for provoking us to explore the facets of giving and create a generous gameplan that benefits not only our world, but us."

**—Julia Bolz**
Founder, Ayni Education International

"John has written an insightful and informative guide for those desiring to live a generous life in service to God. The book's testimonies give insight and direction to anyone getting started on the road to generous giving."

**—John and Barb Findley**
Vine and Branches Foundation

"Our society struggles to maintain strong community born out of deep caring for others. John Stanley offers a timely book, rich with stories and vision, and assembled with the warmth and wisdom of a long-time practitioner."

**—Alan Marty**
Managing Director, Legacy Venture

"While the Gameplan is about generosity, this brilliant author extends the meaning of generosity far beyond the traditional boundaries of sharing material resources. For John Stanley, generosity is a way of life with others in which intangibles such as friendship, values, and vision are shared gifts. This is essentially a profoundly spiritual monograph that will stretch the heart of everyone who reads it. And we recommend it to everyone."

**—Harville Hendrix, Ph.D. & Helen LaKelly Hunt, Ph.D.**
Authors of *Making Marriage Simple*

"We found *Connected for Good* spiritually elevating and insightful about the deeper longings of our human nature. It is motivating both for those who serve in nonprofit work, for those who want to be supportive, and for everyone who wants their life to count for good."

**—B.J. and Sheila Weber**
Founders, New York Fellowship

"This work is a heartfelt guide to emphatic giving for those wanting to do more. *Connected for Good* looks to the soul before the ledger and uncovers the transformative power of passionate and fulfilling charity at all levels, big and small."

**—Thomas R. Livergood**
Chief Executive Officer, The Family Wealth Alliance

"Anyone focused on business as usual with charitable giving and volunteering should read *Connected for Good*. John Stanley calls us all to push the refresh button on how we see generosity for ourselves, our family, and our community."

**—Mark Sabljak**
Publisher, *The Business Journal,* Milwaukee

"John Stanley has a passion for generosity and for the generous life, which he has expressed beautifully in his new book, *Connected for Good*. Readers can learn much from his experience working with numerous donors."

**—Chuck Stetson**
CEO, Let's Strengthen Marriage, National Marriage Week USA

# CONNECTED

## — FOR —

# GOOD

**A GAMEPLAN FOR A GENEROUS LIFE**

# JOHN STANLEY

**CONNECTED FOR GOOD**
A Gameplan for a Generous Life

FIRST EDITION
Copyright © 2013 John L. Stanley

Published by Beacon Publishing.

ISBN 978-1-942611-18-9

Design: Shawna Powell

Printed in the United States of America.

## Table of Contents

I have been put on this planet

to be Josie, Chester, and Ed's son,

Anne's brother,

Jamee's husband,

and Karen and Micah's dad.

It is to these loved ones that I dedicate this work.

# Introduction

When we give well, we build connections. Our attention, our efforts, and our money create bridges to other people and to the world around us.

But what kind of connections are we building? Are they an inch wide and a mile deep or a mile wide and an inch deep? Do they come from the heart or from habit? And are they connections for good or connections for networking?

If you're like me, you want your giving to matter, and you want your connections to be mutually nourishing and make an impact. You know that generosity rightly understood is transformational, not transactional. So how can you make this kind of generosity happen?

## Jim and Lauren's Challenge

Jim and Lauren have ideas about how they want to change the world.

As a couple, they are keenly aware of their blessings—long, healthy lives, a strong marriage, a successful family business, ample net worth—and they want the same prosperity for others. They see much work to do to address poverty, unemployment, and education, to support healthy families, thriving kids, and vibrant communities, and they have a growing sense of urgency to get it done.

For years, Jim and Lauren focused on their children, making sure they got a good start. Now their three daughters are out of the house, taking on lives of their own. Sometimes they do well, and sometimes they hit the inevitable speed bumps along the way, making Jim and Lauren pause and wonder: *Will they be OK?* Their kids' decision-making, relationship choices, and priorities are curious to them. Still, this empty nest phase has freed up the couple's time and energy to turn outward toward their community.

When it comes to giving, Jim and Lauren have much to draw on. Thanks to their thriving car dealership, they have built up an abundance of relationships and resources over time. They have friends in prominent companies and nonprofits throughout the city, and their financial future is secure. Jim is a gregarious connector with a head for numbers, and Lauren has a passion for child development and the arts and is gifted with great organizational skills.

Jim and Lauren have always been exceptionally charitable with their family and neighbors, and they give to organizations that matter, especially to projects that improve their community and to international relief efforts. They can be counted on to arrange events, host, and contribute to others' causes as well as their own. They've held nearly every volunteer position at their church in the last 30 years.

And yet, they can't always do as much as they'd like. They get constant requests for money through the mail, by phone, and in person. Because of their sheer number of board and committee obligations, Jim and Lauren both say no to new opportunities that they would love to say yes to under different circumstances.

More than that, Jim and Lauren can feel the difference between giving with charitable intent and giving from an abundant heart. When they squeeze volunteering into their schedule, give away old possessions, or write checks using their excess financial capacity, they are being charitable. Charity is certainly a good thing, but at the end of the day, they have less than they had before. Their charity sometimes takes a defensive posture: *protect what we have and share what is left over.*

Jim and Lauren know that they've made a difference. They get letters of appreciation from community organizations and personal thanks from people who've benefited from their gifts. Reflecting on their total amount of charitable giving and volunteering, they know that at least half of it is effective—they just do not know which half!

And have they created real change? Children in their city are still poor, families are still broken, high school graduation rates are dropping, and people are still dying of preventable diseases around the world.

For Jim and Lauren, the culture and social fabric of their community, as well as the nation, show signs of cracking, compelling them to stay connected and involved in their church and other nonprofit organizations. However, as the reasons to be engaged grow, their belief that they can really create meaningful change diminishes. They begin to think: *We are doing pretty well, but how can we possibly put a dent in these problems?* They wonder: *Even when we do act, are we really doing much good?*

Jim and Lauren know in their hearts that bigger giving is not better—better giving is better. At the same time, *giving back, paying it forward,* and *digging deep* have become clichés, a call for more of the same.

> Jim and Lauren know in their hearts that bigger giving is not better—better giving is better.

Jim and Lauren want to take their generosity to the next level. They want to create a legacy of true change, to leave the world better than when they found it. But they also want to get more satisfaction from the way they give.

Jim and Lauren's challenge is to be more generous and find more fulfillment in their generosity.

The way that they—and you!—respond to this challenge couldn't be more important.

## Growing in Generosity: My Personal Story

I have many friends and clients who feel as Jim and Lauren do. I've seen the discouragement, disillusionment, and even cynicism that creep in after many years of charitable giving and volunteering. I saw it inside the nonprofit world during my service as a YMCA executive, and I see it now as an advocate and advisor for donors through my consulting firm, The Legacy Group.

And when I see that generosity fatigue, I am unsettled because I know what can be accomplished when we who've been blessed with abundance connect our generous impulses with what we care about most. I know that we can learn to give abundantly in a sustainable way and make the kind of impact we're longing for.

As you'll see, becoming more generous has been a lifelong mission of mine.

Growing up, I was on the receiving end of a great deal of help. My grandparents taught me to work hard at the store they ran in a little west Texas town. The motto of Stanley's Army Surplus was painted on their truck: "We buy, sell, and trade for anything that don't eat!" We sold used clothing, tools, and hardware to farmers and poor migrants who were picking cotton, and my grandparents introduced me to everyone who came in. "This is our grandson John. He's such a good worker!"

I learned early on about giving from my mother, Josie. I heard stories about how she joined the war effort in Britain by enlisting with the Land Army and then the Women's Auxiliary Air Force, where she was one of the earliest radar specialists tracking Allied and German fighters. She was manning the radar on D-Day from the white cliffs of Dover. Then she threw in her lot with an American soldier, married him (they'd spent only twenty-one days together in a year-long courtship!), and traveled to Texas carrying all of her possessions in one suitcase.

Life wasn't easy raising two kids and supporting the family business, but things got more challenging when my father, Chester, died of lung cancer. I was five and my sister, Anne, was ten. My mom moved us to Dallas and enrolled my sister and me at St. Monica Grade School. Just like that she was volunteering and nurturing the kids there and working her day job at Southwest Airmotive. I watched her accept rides to work, church, and the grocery store from her neighbors and return the favor with her only resources: kindness and hospitality. Even though we were living economically on the edge, I never felt deprived because she always seemed to have enough to share.

My mom decided that I needed male influence—I suppose to keep me from becoming at risk—and the Young Men's Christian Association (YMCA) was her solution to a little boy with no daddy. So she arranged for me to go to summer camp on a scholarship. I didn't know it at the time, but I was the beneficiary of a charitable gift someone made to Camp Grady Spruce.

The YMCA, in turn, gave me a sense of confidence through camp counselors and group experiences during those summers. "Boy, you're a leader," they said. *I am?* "Yeah, man, you're a leader." You can only hear that so often before you start acting like it's true. I ended up working part-time at the local YMCA during high school and then through a college internship. I went to a few meetings with the executive director, who introduced me to some higher-ups as a soon-to-be graduate. "Send me your resume!" they said, and I got hired at the Northeast Branch of the Fort Worth YMCA as program director.

I had never reached my academic potential in school, despite the Jesuits' effort, but they did instill in me a dedication to being a man for others. I leveraged this life lesson in my work, and this first real job was no exception. I was running day camp, youth sports, fitness, tennis, swimming, and any other program my executive director, Scotty Morrison, wanted. When Jazzercise was becoming popular in the mid-70s, Scotty said, "We want an exercise class for women using music. Figure it out." So I put together a cassette tape of John Denver and the Beatles and led calisthenics with twenty women for six weeks—a mercifully short-lived assignment for me!

I was also getting to see the inside workings of a charitable organization. I noticed that some of the youth coaches and volunteers were amazing, and some of them were marginal at best. I saw board members who were checked out and disconnected, and others who you couldn't get out of the building.

Fast-forward twenty years to my biggest generosity challenge yet. I was the Chief Executive Officer of a large independent YMCA camp in Wisconsin, the third director in seventy-five years and the first who had not grown up there. The camp gave a chance to a Texan outsider, and I got to sprout my wings as a leader and entrepreneur. This was the 1990s—if you couldn't succeed in the US nonprofit world at that time . . . well, let's just say the economy was roaring, people wanted to be involved, and we were having a fabulous run.

But at the same time, we were dealing with a leadership deficit from camp counselors to full-time staff. Recruiting from the outside was failing to meet the high caliber of leaders required. We needed a way to grow our own and help take the organization powerfully into the future. First we developed a Collaborative Leadership Model, training teachers and high school students across the Midwest. Over time, the model extended the summer camp into a year-round program. The program's success in turn created a demand for leadership training facilities, a development that could house a hundred people and had ample active indoor space since we programmed in the six months of deep Northwoods winter.

At this point, the camp was 80 years old and had never received a gift of more than $100,000. Where were we going to find the $4 million we needed for this project? It was time to challenge the Board, re-engage alumni, and reach out to friends and businesspeople I had relationships with. Three months into the fundraising effort, I was about to present to the campaign committee a $1 million pledge from a very good friend who believed in me and in the future we were building for the camp. Five minutes before the meeting, another friend from Las Vegas, who had earlier been involved in the visioning process, let me know that he and his family would be pledging $2 million. There was a wonderful but awkward moment when I realized that one friend was getting upstaged by the other, so I pulled these two guys aside and said, "I don't know why the Holy Spirit is doing this, but let's announce your pledges as a powerful team effort." It was an amazing and inspiring moment for the donors and our Board.

The Manito-wish Leadership Center and Smith Leadership Village are now signature facilities in the Wisconsin Northwoods, and my daughter, Karen, who is deeply engaged in her own YMCA career, continues her involvement there. My friends helped me turn my love of generosity into a legacy of leadership and now my daughter stays connected to it—what a privilege to be part of this succession.

Still, in 1997, I looked around the room at a Directors' conference and realized that I didn't want to be a YMCA director when I was fifty. My entrepreneurial yearning was bubbling up. Where was I to take this fascination with generosity? Many times, when I sat in my board members' offices, the conversation turned to their corporate and family giving, and they wanted my counsel. Because of my years on the fundraising side of things, I had a good picture of the landscape, and I could advise them on their options.

My friend John Findley was selling his family's company, and he included me in his close circle of friends who provided advice and counsel. I was with him as he navigated the transition. When he and his wife Barb wanted to start a foundation, I journeyed with him in creating The Vine and Branches Foundation. All of this connected to the stirring in my own heart, and with the support of my wife, Jamee, who was (and is) an amazing partner on this journey, I crafted the idea of a consulting and management company providing philanthropic advice and foundation management. I founded The Legacy Group in 1999, and The Vine and Branches Foundation came on as my first client. Since then, we've counseled many generous individuals and families and helped them navigate purpose and bring meaning to their means.

I started on the path of generosity because of the example I learned from the people who raised me: my grandparents, my mother, and my stepfather. I stayed on this path because I kept finding new ways to give and I saw the good that resulted. And now I steer other people on this path because that's the best way I know to change the world.

> The hungry child, the abandoned animal, and the needy student—they all call for our limited capacity.

## An Awakening in the World of Generosity

People who desire to be more generous have a growing sense of urgency—they know there is much work to be done to change the world for the better. Jim and Lauren and others like them want to step up and make a significant impact. They're no longer content with their charitable giving and volunteering—they want to give and act from abundance.

Today, we have access to a 24/7 news cycle, especially as the world is now on a screen in our pocket, purse, or briefcase. The hungry child, the abandoned animal, and the needy student— they all call for our limited capacity. With every click of a mouse, we are confronted by the pressing needs that affect our planet.

At the same time, technology is also increasing our ability to respond to these urgent needs. With flash giving, triggered by national or international disasters, donors can collectively give large amounts in a short period of time over the Internet. This technology means that it's easier to make a contribution and easier to find information when making a decision. Giving USA reports that charitable giving in America increased 4.0 percent in 2011, even in the face of well-publicized economic instability at home and abroad.

As a whole, we are using these opportunities to organize ourselves in communities of common interest or worldviews, and we are reacting to the breathtaking speed of major societal shifts. We are forming groups or tribes whose members believe that the solutions to the problems we see are economic, moral, religious, or political. Then we answer to a variety of niche challenges, such as urban, rural, international, or education issues.

We even see high-profile philanthropists like Bill and Melinda Gates and Warren Buffett pledging to donate most of their fortunes to charitable works, inviting others of wealthy means to follow suit. Still, not many accept the invitation—a 2012 study from *The Chronicle of Philanthropy* shows that the country's wealthy are giving a smaller proportion of their income compared to their less affluent neighbors.

Finally, despite all of our technological advancements, giving and volunteering over the last decade haven't eradicated the increasing challenges that lie before us. The Census Bureau reports that the poverty rate in the USA reached 15.9 percent (48.5 million people) in 2011—its highest level since the 1960s. While divorce rates in America have been dropping among the highly educated and affluent, among the poor and moderately educated, marital satisfaction is falling and divorce rates are going up. According to the National Marriage Project, cohabitation is often the choice, as lifelong marriage seems impossible. The World Health Organization found that 6.9 million children died worldwide in 2011 before reaching the age of five, and more than half of those deaths were from preventable diseases.

> We need a new gameplan for generosity.

Now is the time to address these imbalances. The largest transfer of wealth in history is underway, with the traditionalist WWII generation passing their assets to baby boomers and their adult children. In addition, boomers themselves have had wealth-building lives and have an opportunity to pass on a holistic model of generosity to their heirs if they can just find a way to do so.

We need a new gameplan for generosity.

### Gaps in Our Ability to Be Generous

I know many people like Jim and Lauren who are bored with their giving or maybe frustrated that their desire to be generous doesn't match up with the action they take. They're worn out from the experience and disappointed with the results of their giving, and that unhappiness is holding them back from doing more.

I see three Generosity Gaps that explain why generous people aren't giving as much as they want to.

**The Action Gap: It's not the right time.**

People facing this gap feel moved to be generous but are waiting for a better moment. They may be paralyzed at the thought of adding one more thing to an already busy schedule. They may be putting off generosity until certain criteria are met in their lives—until their children graduate from college, or their business is sold, or they hit a strict financial benchmark. They may not have time to research where their gifts are most needed. They're hoping that others will make up for their shortfall.

**The Accumulation Gap: I don't have enough.**

People facing this gap see a world of challenges and scarce assets to meet those challenges. The fear of losing ground with their current financial standing and that of future generations is too great, so these folks are fractionally generous at best. They wonder whether they will ever be prosperous enough to give lavishly. They can't properly see what they do have and don't know how to give without a sense of loss.

**The Gratification Gap: I might be making a difference, but I'm not seeing lasting change.**

People facing this gap wonder whether their generosity really matters. They give their time or financial resources but can't resist feeling pessimistic about the effectiveness of their efforts. Rather than give up being generous as their pessimism grows, they rationalize the feeling away as the cost of being considered a good person. This group is populated with volunteers and philanthropists on the brink of burnout and disillusionment who ask themselves, *Is this all there is to generosity?*

Here's the clearest way I can explain what it means to want to create change instead of just making a difference. You've probably heard the story of the old man who was walking along the beach and came upon on a young girl darting about in the sand. When he asked what she was doing, she pointed to the starfish lying stranded and said, "The tide is going out. If I don't throw these starfish back in the water, they'll die in the sun." The man looked at the expanse of beach, all the starfish littering the sand, and said, "There are too many. You can't possibly make a difference." The girl bent down to pick up a starfish and threw it back into the ocean with a splash. "I made a difference to that one," she said.

There are many versions of this story[1], but this one is used to reassure philanthropists and volunteers that, even if their efforts only impact one person, their work still has meaning: *they are making a difference.*

However, people who are experiencing the Gratification Gap are not satisfied with making a difference to one starfish. They want to save the whole beach. They want to make sure that this problem of dying starfish is eradicated. They want to go upstream on an issue and solve it once and for all instead of giving to short-term solutions. They want to see *lasting change.* These Generosity Gaps arise because we have been trained to see and practice the basics of generosity without imagining all that we are capable of. We only notice our superficial and limited reasons for giving—because we have to, or we've always done so, or we want to pay forward our blessings. And we think of the resources we have to give—our time, money, and skills—in very constrained ways. How can we take our practice of generosity to the next level?

### A Fresh Playbook for Generosity

There is a better way to give, and it starts with our hearts' desire to connect with God and others in a meaningful way.

God has wired us in such a way that we run best on renewable energy sources generated in relationship. When we see God in the hearts of others, when we build bridges within and across tribal lines, this energy multiplies as it moves from person to person:

- **Engagement with others** happens through working, talking, and playing together.

- **Encouragement from others** comes when they see and affirm what we offer to the world.

> God has wired us in such a way that we run best on renewable energy sources generated in relationship.

- **Transformation by others** occurs as we become wiser, more compassionate people.

The old paradigm of check writing and volunteering can feel exhausting and futile when it lacks the connection that our hearts crave. But building in connection turns our time, talent, and treasure into renewable currencies in the form of **relationships, strengths**, and **resources**.

- **Giving away our relationships fosters community.** For example, when we build bridges between two people for their benefit rather than ours, encourage a young person by being a consistent voice of truth, or help a minority business owner get going by mentoring her, we generate relationship capital. Bonds are strengthened and love can flow more freely.

- **Giving away our strengths allows us to encourage.** We can begin with bringing authenticity and attention to the time we spend with others—our unique presence is a gift that matters. When we do volunteer, giving away our unique skills and strengths creates value for ourselves and for those with whom we share our strengths.

- **Giving away our resources challenges us to grow and be transformed.** When we are already spending with our relationships and strengths, the way we give time and money is forever changed. Now we see where our gifts will have the most impact, and we give from a sense of abundance.

These generosity currencies are powerful because they are grounded in love of God and love of others. Rather than giving from guilt or obligation, we are giving from our heart's desire to connect with God and others in a meaningful way—divine love has nothing to do with performance or altruism. When we practice this kind of love, we are not trying to impress those around us or express our pity for those less fortunate. Instead, we are bringing our whole selves into life, and we are demonstrating our care and empathy for the world around us.

Discovering our heart's desire for connection and spending these currencies on our desire produces stunning results. No longer will we feel fear, anger, or shame around our generosity. Instead, we will discover these rewards in giving:

- **Richer relationships:** Our interactions are deeper and more satisfying.

- **More gratifying acts of service:** When we spend our strengths, we experience the exhilaration of being valued and the joy of doing what we love.

- **More effective philanthropy:** When we are engaged and intentional in our giving, the projects we invest in have a deeper impact. We make sure of it.

Imagine every dollar, every hour, and every solution you offer being multiplied when given in sync with your heart's desire to connect. Generosity so conceived is no longer a stand-alone virtue prodding us into volunteering more time, signing over more checks, or giving away more possessions. This abundant generosity is transcendent in that it reaches into our personal history to bring forth the best we have to offer selflessly to others. It is also transformative in that each act of generosity brings us closer to the fulfillment of our unique purpose in life and more like our true selves as God intended us to be.

> Generosity so conceived is no longer a stand-alone virtue prodding us into volunteering more time, signing over more checks, or giving away more possessions.

## The Generosity Gameplan

In entering this new arena of generosity, it helps to have a gameplan—a strategy mapped out that guides your decisions and allocates your currencies (relationships, strengths, and resources) in the most desirable places.

The Generosity Gameplan evolved from my understanding of strategic planning with nonprofits. Many times I went through this decision-making process with board members about what was important to the organization and how we would go about accomplishing our mission. Essentially, we were doing business planning with an eye to our deep purpose.

When I began hearing the thoughts and desires of philanthropists about how they wanted to change the world, I realized that individual donors could gain just as much clarity and impact by going through a planning process. I started to come up with questions and tools to draw these important guiding principles out of heart and head. *What do you care about and why? What headline causes you discomfort?* Then I helped people identify the best way to make change happen.

### Explore your heart and history

In order to connect and give from your heart's desire, you must know yourself and your heart well. What life experiences have shaped you? What values do you strive to embody and how do they affect your decisions? What are your personal and professional goals? What causes have lit a fire under you? How does your personal story affect your outlook on the world? Is there a greater purpose for your time on earth?

### Count your currencies

To direct your resources toward the things you care about most, you must know what you have to give:

- What **relationships** form your network of business, social, and family ties?

- What **strengths** are inherent in your personality, and what skills have you developed through practice that can help others?

- What **resources** of money, time, space, and possessions can you leverage to do good?

> The Generosity Gameplan ensures that your whole self is involved in making decisions about giving, not just your inner accountant.

### Get in the game

With an understanding of yourself and your currencies, you're ready to take action. You can move with clarity and confidence when your generosity plays are mapped out ahead of time. You can give from a sense of abundance because you appreciate the range of assets at your disposal. And you'll get a boost in energy because you're giving what comes naturally to the people and causes that are most important to you.

In financial terms, the three most common strategies that come out of a Generosity Gameplan are to make strategic contributions, create a foundation, or start a nonprofit. But because we look at giving the currencies of relationship and strengths first, the money is a natural outflow of that. There's no need to reach for a tithing formula to dictate how much to contribute. Instead, your heart prompts you to give.

I have seen that when a philanthropist just gives money, the satisfaction lasts for a short time. But when her feet follow her money—when she tracks where the money goes, promotes the organization, sits on the board, or meets the beneficiaries of her gift—the satisfaction is more profound. The Generosity Gameplan ensures that your whole self is involved in making decisions about giving, not just your inner accountant.

## Who Is This Book For?

The approach to generosity that I describe in this book doesn't depend on how old you are or how much money you have. The principles of giving from your heart's desire, spending the currencies of relationships, strengths, and resources, and multiplying the effects of your generosity can be applied at any stage of life and from any income level.

However, I have written this book particularly for *people of means and substance,* as I call them. Men and women with financial assets, robust social networks, advanced education, and business experience have certain needs related to giving. Drawing on my experience in the world of nonprofits and fundraising, I have tried to serve those needs within these pages. And because of what I believe, my approach speaks most clearly to people of faith.

Most of my clients have a net worth in the millions to billions and volunteer eight or more hours a month. Many of them have a donor-advised fund or a private foundation from which they give. They have headed successful companies or had stellar careers. They often come to me because they find themselves with more time to devote to philanthropy now that their children have moved out of the house or they have retired or sold their business.

> My heart's desire is to connect with people of means and substance who want to maximize their generosity and pass that heritage on to their children.

I am following my own Generosity Gameplan here, knowing that my heart's desire is to connect with people of means and substance who want to maximize their generosity and pass that heritage on to their children. You'll hear stories in the book from just such people, some of whom are my friends and colleagues, and some of whom are clients of The Legacy Group. I trust that these stories will inspire you as to what's possible when you take your generosity in hand instead of just responding to the requests of others. Do you have dreams of doing good in the local, national, or international arena? You may be closer to realizing those dreams than you ever imagined.

This book will show you how to recognize and close your Generosity Gaps by developing a Generosity Gameplan. I'll walk you through the limitations of how generosity is traditionally done, teach you a more heart-centered, donor-led approach to giving, and provide guidance to sketch out your strategy for where to spend your currencies.

This book can be particularly useful for couples searching for something meaningful to do together. Crafting and acting on a Generosity Gameplan is a creative and engaging process that will reveal more of yourself and strengthen your bond with your spouse and those you help as a team.

I look forward to building a bridge with you through the ideas and actions suggested here. With a clear gameplan for living generously, more and more of us will be connecting for good.

# Part I: The Generosity Gaps

Jim and Lauren have always given to charity and volunteered at their church and their girls' school, but somehow their giving is not yet aligned with their personal growth, business success, and social connections.

Jim especially has been stuck between the charitable demands of being a business owner and his personal longings to change the world. He decided long ago that he would do what he was called to do because he was a community leader and that he would focus on what really mattered to him later, maybe when he sold his business.

At one point, Jim served on six charity boards, and he and Lauren were chairing the church capital campaign at the same time. When the economy softened and the demands of the business increased, he was forced to resign from many of his charitable commitments, just when they needed his leadership the most. During this period, he vowed to avoid getting so overcommitted in the future. It was not good for him, his family, his business, or the nonprofits that were getting only a fractional part of him.

Jim and Lauren are also realizing that, after years of giving in reaction to requests, they don't find their charitable giving and volunteering very fulfilling. What really matters is to be generous now, rather than later, and create the sort of change that they see their community and the world are yearning for.

They want to get excited and be changed by their giving.

In Part I, we'll explore why Jim and Lauren are feeling stuck and how they can get moving again to live the generous life they envision.

# Chapter 1

# Why Do You Want to Be Generous?

You want to be generous.

You may not use the word *generous*—perhaps it strikes you as grandiose or self-congratulatory—but still, you have a desire to give of yourself and what you have.

Where does that desire come from? How do we grow from infants who only care about our own needs to adults who care deeply for others? When do we decide that we have enough to share? How do we make the shift from accumulating for ourselves to giving away?

## My Early Foundations in Generosity

Many of us go back to our childhood to answer these questions. I grew up watching my parents and other adults around me practicing generosity. I told you a little about my mother, Josie, in the introduction. My stepfather, Ed Toogood, was also a great example to me.

### Giving His Presence: My Stepfather's Story

Ed's generosity wasn't always expressed in money. Young adults just starting their lives today make more money than he made in his last year of work (he was a middle manager for a national credit company). When it came to money, Ed lived a life of thrift. I remember spending time in his study and watching him work in his accounting ledger with a pencil. He would use that pencil within an inch of its existence, and I always teased him, "Dad, do you want me to loan you some money so you can buy a new pencil?"

"No," he would say. "There's plenty of lead left in this one."

After Ed died, we discovered a 40-year-old box of pristine Ticonderoga pencils in his cabinet. Yet on his desk were eight pencils that he had sharpened to nubs. His pencils fully served their use and were not discarded before they were finished, just as he himself fully served his purpose until his final days at age 92.

When we started our lives together, Ed Toogood had been a bachelor for 45 years and I was a 12-year-old kid. He had no experience being a dad and I had no experience being a son to a man. But that didn't stop us from trying. At that age, I loved to fish by myself, walking the creeks, so Ed invited me to go on our first trip, fishing in the Gulf of Mexico. We drove down to the coast of Texas and stayed in a very seedy hotel. Out on the boat, we had a fun day catching a few red snapper, and then we bought a few more from the market to take home to Mom.

> He had no experience being a dad and I had no experience being a son to a man.

Another time, we tried going camping, but Ed had no camping gear except for old Navy sleeping bags designed for the Arctic—and we were in Texas! We went out to Possum Kingdom Lake, by YMCA Camp Grady Spruce, and what an experience it was. We never went far from his Buick, sleeping at a rocky campsite with no tent and cooking hobo dinners in aluminum foil over the fire. Neither of us had memories of father-son bonding, but Ed was showing me that he wanted to spend time with me, even if he was still learning to be a dad.

I still have the letter he left on my dorm-room desk when I started college, six years into our relationship. He covered four pages with his handwriting, telling me I was starting a new life on my own, encouraging me to "stand on your own hind-legs, express your opinion and do what you *know* is right!" He explained that when he nagged me and expected a lot from me, he was only trying to help me become a better man. Of course, he couldn't resist telling me that I would need a lot of self-discipline for heavy studying! But to have him write, "I couldn't ask for a better son than you, and I wouldn't trade you for anyone" was quite a gift to me.

Long after college, when I was succeeding as an adult in my YMCA career, there came a day when Dad said he was proud of me. If you asked what moment I became his son, this is the one I would point to. So much of what I've learned about generous relationships started with watching Dad give me his presence by paying attention to me, showing up, and telling me how he felt about me.

## A Man for Others: My Youth Leader's Story

I also had some formative lessons about generosity in the church. In high school, I was dating a young woman who belonged to the local Church of Christ, and I joined her church youth group. One day after mass, the youth leader at my home parish, Father Don Fischer, came up to me.

"I understand you're learning a lot about youth groups at your girlfriend's church," Father Don said to me. "I wonder if you'd come and teach our group about what you've been learning?"

Looking back I can see what a clever ploy this was. Father Don didn't scold me for going to another church youth group (as my mother had no doubt asked him to do). Instead, he appealed to my desire to be generous with my knowledge so he would have a chance to mentor me. And it worked. I did talk to the Catholic Youth Organization (CYO), and when my girlfriend and I broke up and I had no more reason to go to that other youth group, I got even more involved at St. Monica. As soon as I joined the CYO, Father Don put me in leadership, and soon I was helping out and recruiting friends to come. He had confidence in me and he made sure I knew it, and that, in turn, increased my self-confidence—a powerful gift to give a teenager.

In many ways, Father Don taught me how to act as a Christian man for others.[2] After CYO on Sunday nights, he and a few others of us would go out for ice cream and talk about how to be in relationship with Christ, the church, and each other. The key seemed to be in connecting to give and receive love. I watched Father Don lead by being present and understanding who I was and what I could do. "We won't ask you to sing because you can't carry a note in a bucket," he said to me. "So why don't you organize?" To this day, he's a man who means so much to me because of the wisdom and care he continues to share with me.

I am grateful to these people and others—teachers, coaches, and bosses—who were able to draw out my strengths. They helped me see how I am gifted. Even my self-reliance, which results in me saying, "I did it myself," was shaped and inspired by God and others. I have been so fortunate to have opportunities to earn and succeed.

I know I'm not the only one who was launched into generosity early on, inspired by people who set a loving example. I've had a great foundation from which to build a generous life.

## What Are Your Reasons for Giving?

As we move into adulthood, some of us pick up more convoluted motivations for giving.

I'd like to look at some of these motivations because, when they go unexamined, they can place limits on our ability to give. These motivations still result in good coming from our generosity, but they can put a damper on our sense of purpose and gratification, which in turn decreases the energy and creativity that could help us give more effectively. See if you recognize yourself in these scenarios.

## Tradition

If you grew up with generosity modeled in your home and church, you may find yourself giving and volunteering out of habit. Your parents always gave 10 percent of their income, so you do too. You started helping with a downtown outreach group in high school and never left. You watched your priest say yes every time someone needed him, and you followed suit.

The wonderful thing about getting plugged into a tradition of generosity is that you develop commitment. You stick with things when it isn't easy or convenient. But the downside is that you may not take time to reflect on how your giving is affecting you and those you're serving. You can get into a routine and not notice problems that arise until they're too big to ignore.

## Obligation

Sometimes an upbringing in generosity can turn into a sense of obligation. You give because you have to. Your family members expect it. Your religion dictates it. Your community assumes you will contribute because of the size of your business and your influence.

You may administer a donor-advised fund or private foundation with minimum distribution requirements. Major donors like Warren Buffett and Bill and Melinda Gates are beginning to exert pressure on other very wealthy people to give away most of their estate, creating a kind of social obligation.

Again, feeling obliged to give can help you maintain commitment. But it can also lead to resentment and frustration at being forced to give when your heart isn't in it. You probably don't do your best when you're just ticking off a box that says Donate or Volunteer.

## Recognition

Perhaps you notice yourself being generous in exchange for the recognition that you get. You may look for a simple thank-you note or for your name on a plaque. You may enjoy receiving an award for community contribution. Hosting a gala fundraiser lets everyone see in person how dedicated you are to supporting a certain candidate or organization.

Recognition encourages you to be willing to put your name and reputation behind the causes you support. There's nothing inherently wrong in being proud of what you've accomplished. But a desire for recognition may get in the way of evaluating the impact of your efforts. And the glow of recognition can be fleeting.

## Social lifestyle

Philanthropy can develop into something of a recreational pastime. Board meetings, organizational retreats, and charity auctions can take up every night of the week and give you a chance to spend time with people you admire. You develop relationships with the people you work alongside and enjoy their company.

Taking pleasure in the social aspect of giving is a good thing, but are the events themselves causing you to overlook challenges at the organizations you support?

## Friend-to-friend

We've all had the experience of giving because a friend asked us to. Social networks are a natural place to turn when raising money because there is already a relationship and goodwill there.

Giving when friends ask can be complicated. You get the joy of helping someone you love as well as the cause they support. But what if that organization isn't really a priority for you—how can you say no and disappoint a friend? Once you say yes, are you obliged to continue giving forever after? Will you be judged on the amount you give? Might you feel that your friendship has been used inappropriately?

Notice that, with each of these reasons, there is **a transactional component to giving.** You get something in return, whether that's the approval and praise of others, the pleasure of social activities, or the reassurance of knowing you're a good person. And while you enjoy what you get, you may not be deeply affected by the experience. (In the next chapter, I'll talk about how generosity can be transformational—how you can be changed along with those who receive.)

> What if that organization isn't really a priority for you—how can you say no and disappoint a friend?

These are also external drivers—they come more from outside than from within. You may need these external incentives in the beginning to help you get past your inhibitions about giving. But as you grow, they can become a hindrance because they don't take into account who you are and what you have to give.

## Reciprocity

There's one motivation I haven't mentioned that is the most prevalent one among people of means and substance. We could call this reason *reciprocity*. You realize how much you've been blessed, and you want to spread that blessing around. You see how good your life is, and you want others to experience the same.

This reason is one that seems to deserve the least criticism. Isn't it selfless to want to share your good fortune? Isn't it a form of justice to help others benefit from your privilege?

Sure it is. I don't deny that. Awareness of our own blessings can lead us to give with empathy and grace. I'm not asking anyone to stop paying it forward or giving back.

But I want us to move beyond reciprocity. There is no possible way to give enough and even things up.

I've learned that there's an even more powerful reason for giving than reciprocity, one that benefits everyone in the equation, that fulfills our heart's desire, recharges our capacity, and multiplies our impact. That reason is to connect.

## Giving to Connect

Isolation is the enemy of generosity. This makes sense when you think about it—if generosity involves both givers and receivers but there are barriers between them, how can meaningful gifts be made? Anything that separates us from others, whether that's institutions, geography, ego, or prejudice, erodes our ability to give.

> Isolation is the enemy of generosity.

**Connection is the healing element that drives isolation away.** Connecting with another person in conversation, with God in prayer, and with ourselves in contemplation reminds us that we were created to live and grow in relationship.

What does it look like when connection is the motivator for generosity?

- You connect with your own ideas and longings for the world, drawing on your personal history and healthy obsessions to find causes that make your heart leap.

- You connect with others whose interests overlap with yours.

- You connect with God by opening yourself to divine inspiration and guidance, trusting that you will find the answers and opportunities that you need and taking comfort that you are not in this alone.

This vision of generosity is not about coming together to sing Kumbayah, but rather about being a powerful source for good. Connecting allows us to do the most effective things in strategic ways and create change instead of simply making a difference. Connecting gives us a deep sense of satisfaction and affirms our value.

> Connecting allows us to do the most effective things in strategic ways and create change instead of simply making a difference.

There's so much more to philanthropy than giving something away. But before I get into all that, let's take a look at the traditional model: giving time, talent, and treasure.

# Chapter 2

# The Limits of Time, Talent, and Treasure

*Time, talent, and treasure* is a very familiar phrase in the world of generosity. These three words describe the range of gifts that are valuable in helping others. We hear *time, talent, and treasure* from university presidents and pastors, relief workers, and directors of our favorite charities. The alliteration of the three Ts makes the phrase memorable and appealing—in fact, it has been in use since at least the 1850s, and it shows no signs of going out of style.

What do we mean when we talk about giving time, talent, and treasure?

- **Time** means hours in your schedule spent working for a cause. When you give time, you are usually doing something that anyone could do, such as attending board meetings, making phone calls, or stuffing envelopes. The emphasis with this currency is on the volume of time you have to give.

- **Talent** means service given from your particular skills and gifts. When you give talent, you are doing something specialized that few others could do, such as bookkeeping, design, or project management. The emphasis with this currency is on the value of the service you provide.

- **Treasure** means money and goods donated to support the operations and initiatives of an organization. As a person of means and substance, you are usually being asked to give more than the average person could give. The emphasis with this currency is often on the size and regularity of your monetary gifts.

In the charitable world (the social sector, as author Jim Collins calls it[3]), the currencies that seem to be most in demand are time and money. These are, of course, very useful and transferable resources, so it's no wonder that they're sought-after.

But talent and other types of treasure may end up overlooked or eclipsed by the simpler appeal of time and money. It takes creative effort to figure out how to use our talents, ideas, belongings, and assets most effectively and for the best result. Neither we nor the organizations that need us are always willing or able to go to that effort. We hear, "Cut the check, please, and don't forget that next Saturday is Volunteer Day."

(Just as an aside, people in the Millennial Generation seem much more clued in to the value of giving talent, partly because they don't have as much money to give and partly because volunteering has become an important part of their recreation, education, and career development. Lessons could be learned from these young people who demonstrate their compassion through their grassroots involvement.[4])

> When you hear the pastor or the social sector leader say, "Time, talent, and treasure," don't you sometimes hear, "Blah, blah, and blah"?

I'd like to be clear—I'm not questioning the historical wording or the real value of *time, talent, and treasure* just to be different or contemporary. The phrase does a good job of communicating that we have much to give. But when you hear the pastor or the social sector leader say, "Time, talent, and treasure," don't you sometimes hear, "Blah, blah, and blah"? Later in the book, I'll suggest some new words to encompass my expanded idea of the currencies we can give, but for now I'd like to explore why the traditional ideas of time, talent, and treasure are holding us back.

## How Do You See Time, Talent, and Treasure?

When you get an appeal for time, talent, and treasure, I know you're inclined to respond positively because of the many motives for generosity that we looked at in the last chapter. You say yes to the nonprofit executive for time on Volunteer Day, and you say yes to the urgent plea for a contribution from your neighbor. You say yes to another invitation to serve on a charity board. You give your credit card number to the relief organization when the natural disaster hits.

When you spend your time and money, an interesting thing can happen: **You feel like you have less than you had before.**

This may seem obvious from a mathematical point of view; if time and money are finite resources and you subtract from your total to make a donation or a volunteer commitment, of course you have less. But I want to emphasize the *feeling* of having less. Perhaps you can bring to mind the moment of exhaustion when you realize how squeezed you are for time in a given week or how tight things are after you fulfill that capital campaign pledge commitment. Do you feel it as uneasiness in your stomach? An ache in your head? A constriction in your chest?

In extreme cases, it may even seem that your schedule or bank account has been hijacked. You find yourself significantly overcommitted and wonder, *How did I get here?*

You're not alone.

Feeling ourselves having less, we are often visited by unwelcome emotions that form the backdrop of our anxiety around giving:

- We feel temporarily vulnerable when we stretch too far with a pledge. How will we respond generously to the next campaign?

- We feel frustrated when we don't see gratitude or lasting change after we give.

- We feel inadequate because we don't seem to be enough or have enough: enough of ourselves, enough clarity of purpose, enough talent, or enough time or money.

How can we avoid swimming in the waters of accumulation, giving away our time and money, feeling the loss, and then getting caught in these difficult emotions? We don't want to stop giving in order to escape the cycle. That only promotes autonomy and results in isolation from God and others. Swimming in the waters of generosity leads to connections and results in care for ourselves and others.

So to explain why this problematic cycle arises and how we can break out of it, I'm going to introduce a few more T words: *transactional* and *transformational*.

## The Cool Nature of Transactional Giving

In business, a transaction is an instance of buying and selling something. There's an exchange of money for goods and services in the marketplace. Usually transactions are impersonal and objective. Both sides of the transaction are theoretically equivalent, and the best transactions are win-win, but sometimes transactions take on the characteristic of "you scratch my back, and I'll scratch yours."

In philanthropy, **transactional giving** can be characterized by this same dynamic of *quid pro quo:* I do something for you, and I expect something in return. A philanthropic exchange may not be as explicit as one in the marketplace, but the transactional nature still affects both parties. Here's how the giver may feel:

- Detached: "I don't know precisely how this gift will be used, but it seems like the right thing to do."

- Resigned: "I suppose I have no choice but to make this gift, since I'm an alumnus and I want to remain involved."

- Calculating: "If I give this, maybe I can influence the organization's priorities."

The receiver may forget about the person behind the gift and focus solely on how that time and money helps reach a goal.

You can also recognize transactional giving when donors are interchangeable and so are their gifts. Does it matter if the dollars come from you or someone else? Does it matter if the person doing the volunteer work is you or someone else? If it doesn't matter, you're likely looking at transactional giving. (I don't mean to be cynical on this point; I just want you to notice how important your particular presence is when you're giving. Are you irreplaceable? This question will come into play when you're creating your Generosity Gameplan.)

> Does it matter if the dollars come from you or someone else?

Think of the CEO of a large company who is serving on 12 nonprofit boards. I've yet to meet a person who has the bandwidth to be personally interested in 12 nonprofits, but I do know many who do this. This CEO is serving by virtue of his position as an executive and his company's large footprint in the community; he's responding to peer pressure that he participate. Those nonprofits get access to his money and his Rolodex, and in return he is admired as a responsive community-minded CEO. What he's doing is not a bad thing—businesspeople have a responsibility to give back to the people who have helped them prosper. But it's transactional. How deep can his engagement be when he's spread so thin? And do the nonprofits really value him as a unique contributor or would they be just as happy with someone else with his wealth and network?

In the church world, it's easy to sit on a lot of committees out of obligation. You feel that you're getting benefit from belonging to that community and that you ought to pay your dues. Clergy and staff can be quite bold in their requests because they're so aware of the constant need for more help. Have you ever walked into a new church and been asked to volunteer even before you decided to join? Ouch. Again, it's okay to volunteer transactionally—that way churches get the support they need to run programs and services. But think how much better it would be to only contribute to faith communities in a way that uses our strengths.

When it comes to donating in a transactional way, **I call that check-writing philanthropy.** Think of the tedium of opening all those appeals that come in the mail, the way that giving to one group gets you on multiple mailing lists. You might write a check just to get the pile off your desk and move on. Maybe you see the charitable receipt when it's tax time, and you can't remember what the organization does or why you donated to it.

Annual campaigns are often transactional. There's a big push for end-of-year fundraising and you're asked to give as much as you can to help an organization meet its budget. Maybe you care a lot about that organization, but in this case you're writing the check because you feel pressured by the deadline.

It can take time for us as donors to realize that what we've been doing is transactional giving. Sometimes we can only see it in the rearview mirror when we realize that giving has become a habit and that our hearts and spirits aren't really involved. Looking at the motives for giving that I explored in the last chapter (*tradition, obligation, recognition, social lifestyle, friend-to-friend, reciprocity*) can reveal the return you're expecting that you may not have been aware of.

For me, the realization came when I switched sides at the table and went from being a YMCA executive who needed money and time from others to being a major donor and grant maker myself. I didn't see it overnight, but my perspective changed pretty quickly. When I listened to a charity leader making a pitch to get a grant from my foundation or one that I managed, I could sense that she was mission-driven and well meaning, yet in some way she was telling me what I wanted to hear, searching for what I was interested in and interpreting her program to match that interest. When people want your money, you're the smartest person in the room, and that's a bad position to be in.

Here's an example: the donor is interested in inner city kids and their success in school. The symphony has budget challenges, so they've added weekday matinee performances for schools. The ticket price is reduced to encourage participation, yet budgets are stretched and schools cannot afford the performance and cannot pass along the fee to the students. Solution: the symphony director says to me, "You are deeply interested in inner city kids; a contribution to support the symphony will allow us to give needy students this opportunity." I wonder, *Is this really what I care about?*

That's when I started looking for a way to transcend the impersonal nature of transactional giving.

And I found it in transformational generosity.

## The Warm Engagement of Transformational Generosity

Before anything is exchanged, you begin to form a connection in order to understand and appreciate the other.

Instead of starting with time or money, **transformational generosity** starts with relationship. Before anything is exchanged, you begin to form a connection in order to understand and appreciate the other.

- **Connecting with God:** Ground yourself in your identity as beloved by God and the knowledge that everything you have comes from God. Pour out your gratitude, longing, and worry in prayer, and listen for a whisper steering you toward the people and places you can serve.

- **Connecting with self:** Reflect on how you see generosity and how you arrived at this understanding. With no regrets, compare your longings to change the world with your actual generous actions. Explore what you have to give and the kind of change that gets you excited.

- **Connecting with people:** Who needs to be appreciated for helping you get where you are? Look around you, opening to old and new friends who may share your interests and desires to help others. Ask questions from a posture of curiosity, and notice when there's a spark of compatibility that you can develop.

When your generosity comes out of relationship, you are engaged with the results of your gift. If you donate to a school and are engaged with the teachers and the students, you see first-hand the impact of your involvement instead of just having them report to you. If you donate to an orchestra and are engaged with the musicians, you understand what performance means to them and to the audience.

There's something I like to say when I advise clients on choosing a charity for their major giving. Assuming that the mission matches your goals, "Back the jockey, not the horse." Leadership matters. Know and back the person or team that is leading, not just the organization. Look to see who's running the deal and who's on the board. For me and for those I advise, we

> A compelling mission, a well-thought-out plan, or a beautiful facility all pale in comparison to the quality of the leadership.

know that there are three qualities of a great grantee: leadership, leadership, leadership. A compelling mission, a well-thought-out plan, or a beautiful facility all pale in comparison to the quality of the leadership.

Ultimately, transformational generosity brings about change and growth:

- **Personal growth:** You learn more about yourself and develop your generous character. You gain confidence about your decisions and your ability to create change.

- **Relationship growth:** Your connections go deeper, and your friendships are mutually beneficial. As you go deeper, you become more aware of others' pain and burdens (which is why many people stay in transactional giving). This awareness opens you up to intimacy and authenticity.

- **Organizational growth:** The charities you work with move further toward excellence and significant impact. They receive larger gifts from serious givers and embrace long-term thinking.

- **Community growth:** Your city, state, country, and planet become more supportive and effective at caring for those in need and for the earth we live on.

- **Spiritual growth:** Everyone you collaborate with has the opportunity to exercise faith and vision.

A friend of mine told me that his consulting business really took off when he stopped seeing figurative dollar signs over the heads of all the people he had lunch with. When he started being present to people with no ulterior motive, no reckoning of what he could gain from the conversation, he actually became more successful at bringing in clients. I've transposed that lesson onto the world of generosity—when fundraisers stop seeing dollar signs over the heads of potential donors, and when donors stop calculating how much they should give and what they can gain, I believe we'll see richer relationships built on trust. And those relationships will lead to more gratifying acts of service and more effective giving.

## Amazingly Ordinary Generosity and Formal Philanthropy

You'll have noticed so far that many of my examples of generosity involve what we know as formal philanthropy: making major grants and serving at the executive level of nonprofit organizations.

I want to take a moment to acknowledge that, within a Generosity Gameplan, there is also room for something called "amazingly ordinary generosity." When Jamee and I first heard Monsignor Don Fischer use this phrase in a homily, we looked at each other and said, "Oh my goodness, this is a keeper." What this phrase means to me is that we all have ways of giving that are as natural to us as breathing, that we would never think to label as *generosity*.

When you take an aging parent to the doctor, when you offer advice at a party, when you help with your child's field trip or invite a friend to stay at your cottage, these acts don't get counted in the statistics and annual reports. But they do play a vital role in your own emotional health and the warmth and closeness of your relationships. Giving like this feels good, and it's a kind of giving I want to recognize and affirm.

Formal philanthropy is not the only, or even the most important, form of generosity, but it will be a major focus in this book. Making major gifts and being a policy-making volunteer are areas that people are drawn to but that some may find intimidating or unknown.

I've been inspired by Adam Meyerson, the president of the Philanthropy Roundtable, and his call for American donors to increase their charitable giving in what he calls the *3 percent solution*. You might be amazed to learn that this country already surpasses the rest of the world in giving 2 percent of GDP to charitable organizations—other developed countries like Britain, France, Germany, Japan, and Canada give 1 percent or less.

As Meyerson writes, "Charitable giving is central to American society. It is the lifeblood of our churches, synagogues, and other religious institutions. It has helped to make our colleges and universities, public as well as private, the best in the world. It is indispensable for the flourishing of the arts, science, and medicine, and the protection of habitat. It provides food for the hungry, care for the sick, shelter for the homeless."[5]

Meyerson isn't content to let us stop there, and he goes on to challenge his audience to imagine what could be done if we raised our total giving to 3 percent of GDP, which would mean an extra $150 billion at the current level of the economy. I am working to support this goal personally and professionally, and I hope this book will impress on you the real possibility that people of means and substance like you can move us toward this target and create real change.

In the next chapter, we'll take a closer look at the world of charitable giving: how it operates and how it needs to change.

# Chapter 3

# Has the Art of Fundraising Been Lost?

There's a frantic, competitive spirit that permeates the fundraising efforts of many organizations. Professionalized tactics from the world of sales and marketing have been adopted to get the most return from the giving public. Annual appeals are well organized, and the folks who are most successful are the ones who tug on the donor's heartstrings with plaintive photos and stories. When charities need major gifts, they research a donor's past giving, network, net worth, and family history in order to make an informed decision on cultivation tactics and who the right peer might be to make the ask. The craft of fundraising is alive and well, but the art—the human connection—is sometimes missing.

As a person of means and substance, you've probably been on both sides of this equation. You know the courting done by nonprofits with phone calls, friendly visits, and lunches out. You've heard directors and major gift officers make a pitch to you or ask you to help get your friends and colleagues to participate. You know the system, and when the appeal matches the donor's priorities, everyone wins. Chances are that you can smell when you're being manipulated—when a fundraiser seems to have a genuine interest in you but is really just interested in your money.

The world of charitable giving could use an overhaul.

> The world of charitable giving could use an overhaul.

The current system accomplishes its aims in bringing in operating, capital, and endowment funds, but as Adam Meyerson points out, the barrier of 2 percent of GDP has yet to be breached. That's because the existing culture of generosity has been hijacked by this system of fundraising, and the level of charitable giving is its primary driver and measure of success. Donors are left floundering in the Generosity Gaps. My aim with the ideas in this book and the Generosity Gameplan process is to propose **a new system where donors take charge of their own giving instead of waiting for fundraisers to ask.** I want to question the status quo and suggest how you can create and direct your own giving strategy instead of simply responding to opportunities that come to you.

To that end, I'd like to pull back the curtain and remind you of a few things about how fundraising gets done in today's climate.

## How Does Fundraising Work Now?

Donors are familiar with the experience on their side of the table: the avalanche of direct mail appeals, the inquiries about estate plans, the professional presentations prepared for foundation boards. But what's happening on the other side of the table?

### *Setting Budgets and Project Targets*

As with any for-profit business, a nonprofit organization needs to bring in enough money to cover its expenditures in order to be viable. A responsible nonprofit prepares a budget that details ongoing and special project costs as well as sources of support like individual donations, foundation contributions, and government grants. This budget is usually drawn up by the executive director and approved by the board of directors.

An aggressive board may set ambitious targets while a more conservative one will play it safe and predict only modest increases over the previous year's income. An organization may have established programs that people depend on and be locked into continuing to fund them, or it may have more flexibility to experiment with new initiatives.[6]

A budget approved by a nonprofit board is not arbitrary but driven by a strategic plan, and while the plan makes clear the organizational direction, the tactics are not set in stone. Boards can be influenced by engaged donors who have a vision for what can be done and by prudent donors who are willing to ask challenging questions.

## Managing Donor Portfolios

When a campaign is planned, organizations have meetings where they identify donor prospects. Perhaps you have been to some of these meetings yourself. Fundraising consultants lead a confidential conversation with the campaign cabinet and ask board members, committee members, and executives about people in their network who may be able to donate. People who know you, know what you care about, and know your business and family history may be discussing you as a potential donor.

In a large nonprofit, the major gifts officers are assigned portfolios of donor prospects. Chances are that there are 100 or more prospects in a portfolio. That's a lot of people to get to know, cultivate, and move from curiosity to engagement in making a gift.

From the major gifts officer's perspective, the smaller the portfolio, the better job he or she can do of cultivating the donor prospects. From the donor's perspective, it's helpful to know that the fundraiser's time and attention are spread over a large group of people and that there are limits to the depth of relationship that can be formed.

You'll know how important a donor you are by the importance of the person you meet with. At a university, for example, you are higher profile if you're meeting with the dean of the school than if you're seeing the alumni director.[7]

*Cultivating Donors and Bringing in Funds*

With a database of donor prospects and their contact information in hand, a major gifts officer sets out to establish a connection, ask for a contribution, and bring in the funds needed to meet the campaign budget.

Fundraisers have taken a page from the playbook of salespeople, and many use software to track every interaction they have with donor prospects. These interactions are called *touches* or *moves*. Donor cultivation is a kind of sales process that takes place in a series of strategic touches. The goal is to foster a relationship between the fundraiser and the donor. Each move is recorded in specialized software, and then the next move is planned: perhaps a thank-you note, an event invitation, or an introduction to the dean. This software does a great job of keeping fundraisers organized, but it also reinforces the fact that you are a prospect.

> Fundraisers have taken a page from the playbook of salespeople.

For example, moves management, a term and system initially developed by G.T. "Buck" Smith and David Dunlop at Cornell University, "is a disciplined process of relationship management that is the best way to assure the maximum return on investment."[8] When a responsible fundraiser carries out this or any other system, it often creates a win-win situation for the institution and the donor. Each move is a chance for the fundraiser to know and understand the donor and look for alignment between what the donor cares about and the organization's goals. I'm sure you can tell when the fundraiser is trying too hard and the discovery process feels like grasping at alignment.

*Compensating Fundraisers*

Fundraisers who abide by the Code of Ethics from the Association of Fundraising Professionals cannot be paid on commission. This is a very important tenet of operation for principled nonprofits, but it may not hold true for the fundraising companies contracted by the local fire and police departments that call you at dinnertime. However, even if fundraisers receive no commission, there is still an indirect relationship between how much money they bring in and how they progress in their profession. Fundraisers care about their numbers insofar as numbers indicate success, keep jobs secure, and support advancement, so fundraisers still have strong incentive to raise as much as possible.

## What Happens When Fundraisers Drive Generosity?

Have you ever heard these sayings?

- "I didn't give because no one asked me to."

- "Every no gets you one step closer to yes."

- And finally (I love this one): "If you build it, they will come."

These three statements and others like them drive much of the social sector ethos today. You know this ethos because you sit on boards and committees and see funding requests that align with these beliefs.

- **"I didn't give because no one asked me to."** This is often true; donors are conditioned to be passive in the traditional fundraising system. But I propose that the generous donor should lead the matchmaking between heart's desire and a charitable cause and not wait until the right fit comes along.

- **"Every no gets you one step closer to a yes."** Again, this is true enough. Fundraisers need to keep up their motivation in the quest for support. But being on the receiving end of this philosophy spells transaction, not transformation, between the donor who cares deeply and the social sector ally who is delivering the program on the donor's behalf.

- **And finally, "If you build it, they will come."** Sadly, this is often not the case. Bob Jenkins, a friend and mentor of mine when I was a YMCA executive, convinced me that donors appreciate *demand-driven* capital improvement and new programs. Prove that there is a demand for the new building or program, and then show that demand to the donor. This lesson from capitalism belongs in the social sector. Enough fields of dreams have been funded.

With every dollar spent and every service delivered, well-intentioned people are making a difference but not necessarily creating lasting change for our neighborhoods and communities.

### Nonprofits Proliferate and Compete

There is no shortage of organizations trying to do good in this country. The number of nonprofits registered with the US Internal Revenue Agency grew by 28 percent between 2000 and 2012. In my county of Milwaukee, the number of nonprofits grew by 75 percent in that same time period. There are now an estimated 1.5 million nonprofits operating in this country.[9]

But despite this boom in problem-solving charitable organizations, the nation's problems are still with us. With every dollar spent and every service delivered, well-intentioned people are making a difference but not necessarily creating lasting change for our neighborhoods and communities. There's got to be a better way.

With this amazing expansion of the social sector, leaders have turf to protect, and a relationship with a donor is part of that turf. "Too soon old, too late smart," I like to say, but when I was a YMCA executive I learned that if I helped my donors give to other organizations that they cared about, they were more generous with my YMCA. It's true. If you love to help inner city kids, you are likely to be generous with the Boys and Girls Club and the urban YMCA. Chances are that the executives of these organizations are competing for your allegiance. No donor I know likes this position, and in fact, most would probably be calling on these two executives to collaborate to create change for the kids they care about so deeply.

I like competition—it inspires nonprofit leaders to do their best and to be effective. But competition in the world of generosity reinforces the belief that resources are limited and keeps people from looking at ways to leverage and multiply their relationships, strengths, and resources.

I have a friend who was asked to resign from an organization where he had volunteered for over 15 years. He was great at hands-on start-up governance, but the organization had now matured. He needed another start-up assignment. The healthy thing would have been for the director to say that she could refer him to other places where his start-up talents would be put to good use. But because she was afraid that she would lose his financial support if he volunteered for another organization, she didn't do that. She lost the support anyway.

## Just Cut the Check, Please

Eager goal-driven fundraisers fill one-on-one donor meetings with endless presentation and too often invite a contribution without knowing a donor's heart's desire. The questions I listen for early in a conversation with a social sector leader are something like "How are Jamee, Karen, and Micah? What sorts of priorities do you have these days, John?" The old adage applies in today's world of autonomy and isolation more than ever, especially in the world of generosity: *I don't care how much you know until I know how much you care.*

Early on, when I was with the YMCA, I didn't pay enough attention to the donor's priorities outside of Camp Manito-wish. I assumed that everyone loved our camp and that it was all donors' top priority. Later, I realized that I might be in the top ten of organizations they cared about. I was part of a portfolio of charities they supported. Again, too soon old, too late smart— when I learned of the other nine in the top ten, it turned out that I knew some of these leaders and could help build relationship bridges and improve outcomes for the donor and my colleague/ competitor.

When is enough enough? Inside an advancement office, the question "How much is enough?" is never answered. That's why your aunt, a widow with a modest portfolio, is taken out to lunch once a quarter by fundraisers at a university. She's already given them an annuity gift, but they think she has more available and they're trying to cultivate the relationship for more through these lunches. Your aunt is lonely and enjoys the attention, but I wonder who is in the driver's seat in that relationship?

Timing is everything, and every major campaign has a deadline, whether it fits into a donor's plan or not. The campaign has a quiet phase when, in most cases, the pace-setting gifts are pledged equaling half of the goal or better. Then a public phase and finally a cleanup phase are executed. The win–win relationships put forward a clear and compelling vision and invite input from the donor that can really affect the plans. Then the donor serves as the navigator on details so that any commitment fits with his or her goals. But all too often, more impactful gifts could have been secured if not for a deadline.

## Economic Change Is Driving Social Sector Change

There's a reason that generosity needs to be done differently at this point in history. The United States was founded during the Agricultural Age, with an economy that was small, local, and independent because of the restraints in place when using wooden tools and animals to cultivate food.

Then, for decades, the Industrial Age shaped our economic structures. Factory production required centralization of labor and resources as well as continued expansion, so this age promoted the growth of cities, increased regulation, and the concentration of capital.

But now we are moving further into the Information Age—the age of the microchip—and economic structures are becoming more open, horizontal, and decentralized again. Farmers became company men, and now company men are becoming free agents. Anyone can reach into a pocket, order goods and services from anywhere on the planet, and have them delivered in a few days. The workforce is much more mobile, and smaller enterprises can have a significant reach.

> Bigger is not necessarily better, but better is better. Organizations that are local, small, quick, and decentralized will hit their stride in this environment.

Just as business and government needs to adapt to the changing economic landscape, so too does the social sector. Sometimes larger organizations can deliver on big ideas because of their capacity and reach, but other times large means less agility and less connection with donors and people being served. Bigger is not necessarily better, but better is better. Organizations that are local, small, quick, and decentralized will hit their stride in this environment. And donors can act more like entrepreneurs, taking responsibility for setting the vision and evaluating the effectiveness of nonprofit efforts.

The Generosity Gameplan process and my work with clients through The Legacy Group supports donors and grant-makers in becoming more like free agents than company men. We want to be searching out organizations with better staff, better programs, better facilities, and better evaluation—organizations that create effective change.

My colleague Calvin Edwards, who is also a philanthropic advisor, got into this line of work because he felt that major donors didn't have the resources they needed to find and qualify good organizations to support. "I wanted to make the philanthropic marketplace much more efficient so that good dollars went to good places," he says. "I saw that some not-so-good places were getting funding because people would take the easy way out and give to a big, well-known organization. Or they'd give out of fatigue, just doing over and over what they always did. Others would say, 'He seems like a good guy,' and give based on reputation without really knowing. In the for-profit world, you have high-rise buildings in Manhattan filled with stock analysts publishing reports, and investors generally buy stocks of good companies because this information is public and available. But we don't have anything that resembles that in the non-profit marketplace. I wanted to be a beachhead of sanity to start to remedy that problem. It's a bigger job than I can do on my own. But that's what motivated me, trying to get people information so they could make informed decisions."

I share Calvin's motivation and his mission to empower people of means and substance in this new climate of technology and entrepreneurship that defines the Information Age. I believe it's an important piece of the puzzle in making sure that our society can ride out these changes while taking care of the planet and its people.

## How the Nonprofit Sector is Changing

We're starting to see some good signs that fundraising and social service delivery are moving in this direction of small, local, agile, and decentralized initiatives. Crowdfunding, for example, has become a way for individuals and small groups to go directly to donors and bring in funds for pressing needs and independent projects. Take a look at the causes campaigning through Indiegogo.com to get a sample of what's being funded by modest, distributed donations.

DonorsChoose.org is another such organization that allows donors to give straight to teachers and educators who need contributions for classroom projects. Opportunity International provides microfinance loans, savings, insurance, and training to over four million people working their way out of poverty in the developing world. A donor can make a loan directly, start a local fundraiser, or engage a friend by giving a gift card.

The Khan Academy, an educational initiative, is accomplishing big things through a small, efficient organization. I first heard of it when the founder, Salman Khan, spoke to a group of 300 philanthropists in Arizona in 2011. The idea to deliver short teaching videos online came out of Khan's relationship with his niece and her trouble with algebra. He went into his closet and recorded some tutorials for her using his iPhone and a white-board, and he was thrilled when she got an A on her next test.

The site has grown to over 3,600 videos that teach math, science, and some humanities principles for the K-12 level. Khan had this crowd of conservative philanthropists completely engaged with his presentation, and afterward five or six people approached him with offers: "Mr. Khan, I'll give you $1 million tonight if you'll do a video series on the constitution." Here's what excites me about The Khan Academy:

- It is small, grassroots, and cheap, and its videos can be distributed on mobile devices.

- It is based on spreading knowledge democratically.

- It increases human capacity, human dignity, and self-sufficiency.

- The founder is someone who is looking further than left and right and who understands the importance of incremental change.

This approach to philanthropy, where donors take charge of their giving, is still emerging. Like the new wine in Jesus' parable, this new way of being generous can't be poured into the old wineskins of charitable giving driven by fundraisers. We need new wineskins, a new relationship between fundraisers and donors that allows us to truly connect and collaborate.

It's no wonder that folks have had difficulty switching from their tried and true habits, the transactional giving that made more sense in the Industrial Age of large, centralized nonprofits. It's no wonder that people are stalled in the Generosity Gaps that arise in uncharted and confusing territory. In the next few chapters, we'll take a look at each of these Generosity Gaps and what's going on in the space between longing and action.

Chapter 4

# The Action Gap

In the previous chapters, I explored these themes:

- How our motives for being generous can be limited unless we call on our expansive inner motive to connect.

- How the currencies we spend (time, talent, and treasure) can lead to a pattern of transactional giving from what's left over, rather than from a posture of abundance that transforms us and our relationships.

- How the charitable giving system is driven by appeals, with fundraisers leading the way and donors reacting and, at times, disengaging.

When these three factors intersect with formal philanthropy, Generosity Gaps appear. The Generosity Gaps hold us captive and prevent us from taking our generosity to the next level by being more generous and giving with greater purpose.

- **The Action Gap:** It's not the right time.

- **The Accumulation Gap:** I don't have enough.

- **The Gratification Gap:** I might be making a difference, but I'm not seeing lasting change.

I've observed these three Generosity Gaps in hundreds of people that I've worked and socialized with over the years. Honestly, it confounds me to meet men and women of tremendous empathy and compassion who have so much capacity, who could create real change with their relationships, strengths, and resources, only to realize that they are stuck and that their generosity is falling short.

I am highly motivated to call out these Generosity Gaps, which can seem as vast and impassable as the Grand Canyon, so that together we can bridge them and cross over to an exciting new practice of transformational generosity.

(There are most certainly other Generosity Gaps than the three I describe here, but these are the ones I find the most pervasive and most detrimental among people of means and substance.)

Let's begin with the first Generosity Gap that has immobilized many of us at some point in our lives: the Action Gap.

## The Action Gap: It's Not the Right Time

*"There are risks and costs to action. But they are far less than the long-range risks of comfortable inaction."* John F. Kennedy

How do you know you're in the Action Gap?

Because you're watching and waiting.

The conditions aren't right to give and volunteer in the way that you want to (or the way you think you should). So you're biding your time until things change:

- When the kids move out of the house, you'll have more time to help out.

- When your youngest is finished college, you won't have those big tuition bills.

- When the business finally sells, there'll be excess capital.

- When you retire in a few years, you can take on some bigger philanthropic projects.

- When your mother moves into assisted living, you'll be able to travel for nonprofit work and conferences.

When I think of the Action Gap, my friend Frank comes to mind. For years, he would say to me, "John, I'm only going to give this much to your annual campaign, but when I die, you'll get a big check." And he was true to his word. After he passed away (much too early), his estate fulfilled his pledge for a large contribution, enough for us to dedicate a building to him. But he never got to see that building or, more importantly, the good it did for kids. His family and I wish that he hadn't waited, and that he could have seen the change he created with his gift.

### What Leads You into the Action Gap?

If you are in the Action Gap, you wait because you believe that giving will be easier or have more impact in the future. You promise yourself that you'll do your part when the way is clear, and you depend on others around you to pick up the slack in the meantime.

The Action Gap emerges during the **busyness** of your earlier years, when you are building a business or career, or when you have young children and are attending to all the demands of family. You may have dropped some of your commitments, intending to come back to them once life settled down. But somehow full schedules only get more jam-packed and doing anything extra seems impossible.

> You promise yourself that you'll do your part when the way is clear.

Sometimes you are stalled because you are **expecting ideal outcomes** from every act of generosity. You want to get involved with a really effective organization—the best in the city! You are waiting to serve on a board that has just the right governance structure, an executive director with a certain *alma mater,* the best facility, and the lowest fundraising costs. You want to establish a foundation that will involve everyone in the family. But you don't think you have the time or money to do things properly at the moment.

Perhaps you feel like you **lack information.** You don't know where to begin when it comes to evaluating nonprofits and navigating the financial and legal questions around making major gifts. You don't know anyone who can help you, and you don't have time to do the research on your own. You don't even know where your money would be most needed. Everything seems too complicated or consuming.

You may also find yourself **running on autopilot.** Without the time and quiet to step back and evaluate your priorities, you're perpetuating a habit of holding back your generous impulses. Perhaps you're staying in a job or a lifestyle that constrains you, but you never think to question it.

You may hide in the Action Gap because you fear what will happen if you try to cross over.

You may be afraid of **over-commitment** if you try to give beyond your current capacity. Most likely you've experienced the fatigue and pressure of saying yes too much, and you don't want to go back there again. You may notice that you have less energy, or you have to be careful about safeguarding your health. You don't want your generosity to consume you, so you keep it at a modest level.

Possibly you fear **mediocrity** in giving. You feel that the donations you could make right now are not significant enough to create the change you want to see. You are concerned that your efforts would be wasted because you can't do the proper research or partner with the right organization. You have a grand vision but don't know how to realize it, or you don't feel you have the capacity to do it justice.

When you are in the Action Gap, you probably don't like to think about generosity too much because it makes you feel guilty or unhappy about not doing more. It's easier to table the subject, pay more attention to the pressing personal needs right in front of you, and hope you can make up for it later.

### What Will Move You Past the Action Gap?

The power of the Action Gap is based on two assumptions about generosity—that giving leaves you with less, and that there is a right way to practice effective generosity that takes a lot of money and effort.

I want to correct these two assumptions and show you more of the true nature of generosity.

**You can give generously without ending up with less.**

When you practice transactional giving, you can become tired and discouraged. Donor fatigue is a very real phenomenon, and it often happens because you are not getting nourished by connection. Money, time, and effort are flowing out, but meaning, energy, and love are not flowing back. No wonder you are fatigued.

As you shift toward transformational generosity, you will be amazed at how your connections sustain you. Even if you are volunteering the same hours and giving the same amounts as before, you will find yourself buoyed up and excited at the end of the day. Rather than dreading the next meeting or commitment, you will anticipate and savor it. God has designed us to operate this way, to be recharged by using our strengths and resources in relationship—in fact, this is a built-in guidance system that shows us when we are serving within our purpose.

**Generosity is not something to check off a list but a way of life.**

This is what I mean by amazingly ordinary generosity. Yes, formal philanthropy is critically important, yet regular, natural acts of giving that we wouldn't even think to call generous play a key role too. When you take an extra moment to hear how someone is doing, when you smile at the cashier, when you tip a little extra, your authentic presence makes the world a warmer, brighter place.

Frank Hanna is a friend of mine who is the CEO of an investment firm and the author of *What Your Money Means and How to Use It Well*. Here's how he describes this principle: "Generosity should not be just a part of my life, but something that runs through every day. For example, there are two ways of staying physically fit: you can go to the gym once in a while and otherwise sit at a desk, or you can stay active and eat well throughout the day. If all year you are selfish, and then once a year you give money to poor kids, that's more absolution of guilt than generosity. It's better to have generosity weave through the way you deal with everything."

> If generosity can be everyday and ordinary, as well as grand and extraordinary, that takes away much of the pressure that we feel in the Action Gap.

If generosity can be everyday and ordinary, as well as grand and extraordinary, that takes away much of the pressure that we feel in the Action Gap.

**You can give differently at different stages of life.**

Your parents encouraged you to give your nickels and dimes when you were young, not because of their monetary value, but because they wanted you to learn that generosity was important and to see how it felt. Think of what your giving and volunteering looked like when you were a teenager, a young adult, a newly married couple, raising young children, starting a business. Every stage was valuable in what you learned and how you touched others.

We need a diversity of contributions to assemble the full spectrum of generosity. We would never discourage school children from holding toy drives and rummage sales just because their gifts are dwarfed by multi-million foundation grants. We wouldn't try to stop seniors from making coffee after church if that's what they can do. So let's not downplay our own efforts, however constrained they may be by our life responsibilities.[10]

**You can give small but make big change.**

Grand projects often turn our heads, but just because they're grand doesn't mean they'll succeed. A little improvement upstream can have a large impact downstream, where the effect of tiny corrections is multiplied. So if you are at a place where your philanthropic contributions must be smaller because of demands in other areas, take heart that they can still be effective.

St. John's telling of Jesus feeding the 5,000 illustrates this principle beautifully. The disciples looked at the crowd, the hunger, and the limited supply of food, and they worried. I imagine the shame that the little boy must have felt when St. Andrew saw his generous gift of loaves and fishes and said, "What good is so little for so many?" And yet Jesus took notice and reversed the put-down, essentially saying: "I'll show you what good this is for so many!" In a simple way, Jesus blessed what food was available and asked the people to do the work of giving it away. Everyone had their fill and abundant leftovers were gathered up.

Our gifts may also seem to shrink in the face of overwhelming need. But we can trust that God will gather and increase those gifts. Notice that the boy's act was truly one of transformational generosity: he was moved to give by his connection to Jesus and the crowd, and the people present to witness this act, along with those who have heard the story since, have been changed by his good-hearted gesture and Jesus' reaction.

## Steps Out of the Action Gap

*1. Decide that you will act before the better time arrives.*

Look around and see what is possible for you now, rather than lamenting what isn't possible. Find out what others like you are doing and take inspiration from their examples.

Do you have young adult children in the house? Could you find a family project to do together—working on homes for Habitat for Humanity, or assembling and delivering care packages for the holidays? Could you start involving your children in the family foundation's philanthropic work?

Are you still heavily involved in your business? How can you leverage your power and influence there for good? What platform could you establish for you and your employees to be generous? Can you be counter-intuitive by being a force for community good with a competitor?

*2. Decide that you will make the better time happen now.*

Acting generous takes a pulse; being generous takes a plan.

Some people have a kind of *carpe diem* moment when their lives are touched by illness, accident, or crisis that convinces them time is short and they need to act right away.

Others realize that they have been following a certain lifestyle out of habit—working full-time, waiting to retire at 65, maintaining a large house, or keeping a full slate of social obligations. When they stop to question those habits, they realize that they really are free to do something different and to follow the call of a more transformational generosity.

Waking up to the opportunities of action now will pay all kinds of dividends. How exciting to think of what you will do when you are no longer watching and waiting. Today is the perfect time to sow and reap.

# Chapter 5

# The Accumulation Gap

We've all felt the pain of scarcity at some point. We've all experienced lack—whether we needed more money, better health, or more love in our lives. And when we're trying to look after our families and ourselves, to protect ourselves from scarcity and loss, it's pretty natural to encounter what I call the Accumulation Gap.

## The Accumulation Gap: I don't have enough

*"As many successful people have discovered, growing your net worth may gain you more money, but it doesn't give you a life."* Bob Buford, in the foreword to *Enriched: re-defining wealth,* by John Sikkema

How do you know you're in the Accumulation Gap?

Because you're worrying.

- You worry that tax dollars and philanthropic largesse will never be enough to fix the world's problems.

- You worry that the economy will get worse before it gets better.

- You worry that you won't be able to support your children the way you want to.

- You worry that some unforeseen disaster will strike and wipe out your business.

- You worry that your life will last longer than your money.

- You worry that you'll never be wealthy enough to give extravagantly.

My friend Ron Jones, who has served on his church stewardship committee for 20 years, described to me a deer-in-headlights look he sees on the faces of some congregants on Stewardship Sunday. These are often widows of means and substance whose husbands handled all of their financial affairs, and being asked to give— even just to give their time and talent—sends them straight into the Accumulation Gap. If you don't know how much is enough, it can be frightening to think about giving anything away. Regardless of net worth, the Accumulation Gap is real.

> If you don't know how much is enough, it can be frightening to think about giving anything away.

## What Leads You into the Accumulation Gap?

There are a number of reasons why you might think you don't have enough, even if you're a person of wealth and substance.

You may have **a past of poverty or frugality.** I'm thinking of my friend John Kasdorf, whose parents grew up during the Depression. His grandfather had been an executive and ended up selling eggs and life insurance door-to-door, and that experience left John's mother with a very thrifty nature. Everything the Kasdorfs had was reused and recycled—John grew up wearing his brother's hand-me-downs and didn't get his first new suit of clothes until he asked for it specifically for middle school graduation. Giving was still a principle of the household, and his parents dedicated money to the church, but John also learned to hoard his share from his two siblings. Many of us who came from modest backgrounds have picked up habits of frugality that are hard to break, even when we become more prosperous.

You may be **comparing** yourself to others who are wealthier. Unless you're Carlos Slim, the Mexican billionaire who is the richest person on the planet in 2012,[11] there's always someone who has more than you. You might tell yourself that you are comparing in order to motivate yourself, to aspire to greater things. But comparison opens you up to a sense of shame where you feel that you are less than that other person who gave a larger gift.

You probably also know **your balance sheet.** You've put effort into growing and managing your wealth, and you take great responsibility for stewarding what you've earned and inherited. No doubt you've heard that people of means in America give away a smaller proportion of their income compared to the less affluent. One of the reasons for this, I think, is that the culture encourages us to stake our identity in money and possessions.[12] Income and net worth define social circle, lifestyle, and reputation, so giving as little as we have to in order to remain in the circle is the unspoken social contract. Dig too deep and you'll upset "the balance of things."

Abundance is a rather temporary gift from God, but it's common to lose sight of this truth, especially when you are a producer and a success in life and the marketplace. A **sense of entitlement** can creep in because you appear to be in control, especially of your money—you are the one who pays the bills, runs the business, calls the broker—and you may begin to believe that money belongs to you, and you are solely responsible for deciding how to use it.

Media is often the enemy of truth. **Never-ending bad news** plays a role in creating a sense of scarcity too. If you're constantly exposed to stories about corruption, bankruptcy, financial crisis, unemployment, and the housing crash, your outlook is affected. While it's good to be informed, the tone of this coverage—the fear mongering that is designed to sell newspapers and TV ads—can make you overly pessimistic about your own prospects.

Again, you get trapped in the Accumulation Gap because of your fears of what's on the other side. Jim Collins, author of *Good to Great,* said in a PBS interview with Charlie Rose that some people are half-full and others are half-empty kind of people. He thinks of himself as a full-to-the-brim person, but the glass could shatter at any time.

Market volatility, delays by policy makers, and changes in the playing field create an **uncertain future** and can be very unsettling. Any accident or catastrophe could change your circumstances overnight, and if you don't know what might happen, how can you be prepared enough to face it? The unpredictable nature of life can make us feel very vulnerable and reluctant to take risks. My friend Gael Romoser is the daughter of an immigrant who lost his life savings and had to rebuild from scratch, and that experience has made her understandably cautious when it comes to making financial gifts.

Perhaps you are most afraid of **letting others down.** You feel you've been entrusted with much, and like the manager who buried his talents in the ground rather than risk losing them and disappointing his master, you've chosen an overly cautious approach. You dread depriving your spouse, children, or grandchildren of anything they need, or disappointing your parents who passed their estate on to you.

Fear of **other people's opinions** can factor into the equation. If the worst happens and it turns out you really don't have enough resources to take care of yourself and your family, you could lose your reputation as a prudent financial manager. Such a loss might feel very public and humiliating, to be avoided at all costs.

### What Will Move You Past the Accumulation Gap?

The Accumulation Gap depends on a misunderstanding of abundance—looking at resources from the earthly, material perspective rather than from the spiritual perspective. Let me share a few insights about knowing what is enough.

**More is never enough.**

The nature of money is such that there is no limit to how much you can accumulate. But accumulation is a funny thing; the drive to get more rarely goes away, no matter how much more you have.

> Accumulation is a funny thing; the drive to get more rarely goes away, no matter how much more you have.

On the other hand, there are ways to plan and answer the all-important question, "How much is enough?" Once this threshold is crossed, there is an immense sense of freedom, because everything else is surplus to be given away.

Jesus famously addressed this concern in the Sermon on the Mount when he reminded us that we cannot add any time to our lives, so why worry about hoarding anything else? Security in this sense is a myth.

**You already have more than enough.**

This chapter has focused a lot on money, because that's the most common way we measure whether we have enough. But that narrow definition is what leads us to the Accumulation Gap. If you widen your vision, you'll see that you have so much more than what you bank: a safety net of relationships, a storehouse of strengths and experience, a deep well of wisdom and ingenuity, as well as an infinite divine presence with you. All of these resources are available to give away, and they will also buffer the blow of any financial setbacks that come your way.

Again, Jesus reminds us that the lilies of the field and the birds of the air have all they need, thanks to a benevolent Creator and an abundant creation, and that we are much more precious to God than these.

**Generosity works best when you go all in.**

As an investment banker, Frank Hanna knows all about the practice of *hedging*—not putting all your eggs in one basket. Hedging in the material world makes sense; when you buy insurance or sign a contract, for example, you're taking reasonable steps to protect yourself if things go wrong. But in the transcendent spiritual world, Frank says, hedging doesn't work: "As soon as you hedge your love for your spouse, the love will be less than it should be. When you hedge your generosity, it becomes something other than generosity." The truth of this hit for Frank when he had his first child—that feeling of being willing to do or give anything, even jump in front of a bus for his daughter. Holding anything back would betray that love.

> "When you hedge your generosity, it becomes something other than generosity."

Abandoning your urge to hedge your generosity takes faith. You don't know that everything will turn out okay or that your gifts will bear fruit. But you trust that God is calling you forward and you jump in with both feet, believing that you will be taken care of.

## Steps Out of the Accumulation Gap

*1. Acknowledge your hunger.*

In their book *Living the Call: An Introduction to the Lay Vocation*, Michael Novak and William E. Simon Jr. encourage Catholic laity to see lives of service differently. I think they have tapped into a hunger that transcends Catholic lay ministry and put it front and center into our lives of generosity. Michael Novak describes this familiar longing: "They want to love their neighbors better, the poor much better. They see around them so much pain, enervation, weariness, dryness of heart, sheer boredom and emptiness. They confront a spiritual desert all around them under the merry-go-round of the luxurious shopping malls—and they feel that desert advancing in their own souls."

We are tempted to ignore this longing, to try to fill it with other things, because we don't believe we can satisfy it. But the only way we can feed our true hunger for doing good is if we acknowledge it first.

### 2. Pursue experiences that create empathy and change heart, head, and horizon.

John Kasdorf, my friend whose parents raised him with Depression-era frugality, says that a light switch came on for him when he began travelling as a young officer in the Navy. "My eyes were opened unbelievably to what the rest of the world looked like," he says. "While I'd been fighting for my share at the dinner table, I never thought about the need that was out there, the poverty in the rest of the world." John's wife, Sherri, had the same reaction when they visited other countries as a new couple: "I always wondered, why do I have what I have? Even though what I had wasn't a great amount, it was more than they had." With an awakened sense of compassion for those less fortunate monetarily, John and Sherri gave simply at the beginning of their marriage, and they continually look for ways to do more, as I'll share with you later in the book.

In its 2012 study "How America Gives," *The Chronicle of Philanthropy* found that people's level of giving had a lot to do with where they lived and who their neighbors were. The study showed that when the affluent are isolated in wealthy boroughs, and when they live outside large metropolitan areas, their proportional level of giving is lower than for those who live in more urban and economically diverse ZIP codes. I think this finding shows that seeing needs first-hand and being aware of financial advantages encourages generosity.

If you find yourself in the Accumulation Gap, I encourage you to move outside your familiar circles. Travel downtown or around the globe, read and watch films about communities and countries in crisis, but most especially, engage with people from different backgrounds and circumstances.

> "Once the question 'How much is enough?' is answered, everything that remains is freedom"—freedom to pursue your generous desires.

### 3. Discern how much is enough.

The task sounds daunting, but it is very doable. Through carefully crafted plans that address your spiritual, emotional, relational, and financial goals, you can begin to realize the generous purpose that is your heart's desire.

My friend Rick Harig, for example, helps people develop purpose-driven plans that address moral, emotional, and social issues and align financial and legal strategies with personal values. Rick is quick to point out that "Once the question 'How much is enough?' is answered, everything that remains is freedom"—freedom to pursue your generous desires.[13]

### 4. Encourage each other to stretch as a couple.

My friend Gael Romoser, whose father lost his savings, is married to a man who is more comfortable with giving. When it comes to making their charitable donations, she and Dave have lots of discussions, walk away and stew things over, and then come back and resolve the decision in a way they're both comfortable with. Sometimes Gael surprises Dave by agreeing to gifts that are outside of her comfort level (he calls them stretch gifts). Other times Dave rethinks his plan to allow for her concerns. I think their approach of give-and-take combined with prayer is a great way to deal with the Accumulation Gap.

In *Mere Christianity,* C.S. Lewis wrote that, "I am afraid the only safe rule is to give more than we can spare. In other words, if our expenditure on comforts, luxuries, amusement, etc., is up to the standard common among those with the same income as our own, we are probably giving away too little. If our giving does not at all pinch or hamper us, I should say it is too small. There ought to be things we should like to do and cannot because our commitment to giving excludes them."[14]

By stretching yourself and walking directly into your fear of not having enough, you are building your faith. By refusing to hedge, you are exercising generosity that can transform you to your very core. We never miss what we give away.

# Chapter 6

# The Gratification Gap

We all want to look back on our lives and see that we did things that mattered. But when we're caught up in the minutiae of every day—dentist appointments and email, daily errands and travel—we can lose sight of that larger sense of purpose. Those who care deeply about their impact on the world but who are unclear about the significance of their giving will likely find themselves in the Gratification Gap.

## The Gratification Gap: I Might Be Making a Difference, but I'm Not Seeing Lasting Change

*"The non-profit institutions are human-change agents. Their 'product' is a cured patient, a child that learns, a young man or woman grown into a self-respecting adult; a changed human life altogether."* Peter F. Drucker, *Managing the Nonprofit Organization*

How do you know you're in the Gratification Gap?

Because you're wondering and questioning.

Effectiveness matters, and you're not sure whether your giving is doing good. You may be saving a starfish or two but you want to rescue the whole beach or, better yet, prevent starfish from ever getting marooned again. So you're asking yourself these questions:

- Does it really matter if I go to this board meeting?

- What happened to that donation I made a few months ago?

- How do I decide which requests to turn down?

- How can I keep giving what I'm giving year after year?

- I feel like I'm just going through the motions. Is this all there is to generosity?

My friend Mike Klonne is someone who started volunteering as a teenager with sports and inner city youth programs. "It was inbred in me," he says, by his mother and the Brothers at his Catholic high school. He continued to be active at varying levels through college and into his 20s and 30s, but reached a point in midlife when he found his personal satisfaction was lagging. "I made a commitment to do more hands-on volunteering in my late 40s, and I got directly involved in a mentoring program. Working with specific inner city youth from dysfunctional families, I felt positive about the influence I was having." Mike knew he was making a difference, but he also saw some bigger problems in public school education that limited his impact. Mike started questioning—was mentoring really enough? How could he help create lasting wide-scale change for the youth he worked with?

### What Leads You into the Gratification Gap?

You wonder about effectiveness because giving is costly and you want to make sure that the gift has a tangible social return on investment. You want your generosity to have some sense of significance for yourself and those you help.

If you are **giving in reaction** to fundraisers and organizers, rather than proactively from your heart's desire, the Gratification Gap is a real danger. The causes you end up supporting may feel random or unconnected to your own history and passions, and you may have less motivation to follow up on results.

You may experience the Gratification Gap because you are **not personally engaged** in your giving. If you are making contributions without meeting recipients face-to-face, or if your volunteering doesn't involve building relationships, you would understandably feel isolated and out-of-touch, unsure of the good you're doing.

Perhaps you are **overwhelmed by requests.** Calvin Edwards, my philanthropic advisor friend, once heard this from a major donor: "I feel like I'm in the middle of a football field during a college game, and everyone is yelling and screaming, and I can't hear the call. There's too much noise." This is a vivid description of what often happens for people of means and substance—so many fundraisers are clamoring for money that you can't work out which ones to go with. Discriminating among all the options is a challenge. Calvin's friend was paralyzed by the noise and held back from giving at his potential.

> "I feel like I'm in the middle of a football field during a college game, and everyone is yelling and screaming, and I can't hear the call. There's too much noise."

Your charitable giving and volunteering may be **spread too thin.** Directing small amounts of time and money to many organizations may seem like a good solution to the problem of too many requests. But distributing your resources everywhere makes it difficult to stay current on the initiatives you're supporting, let alone cultivate personal connections. Spreading yourself thin makes you susceptible to donor fatigue and volunteer burnout.

You may be **unaware of your impact.** Perhaps you can't keep track of all the reporting material that comes in, or you have no way to evaluate whether an organization has made good use of its funds. You may hear individual stories but wonder about the wider systemic changes. You may not know what questions to ask, or your beneficiaries may not know how to answer them. I often see a black hole effect when people are giving to general operations, which includes paying overhead, repairing the roof, replacing vehicles, and other maintenance. You may feel like your money is disappearing into a black hole because the expenses never end and it's much harder to see how they support the direct work of the organization.

What fears keep you in the Gratification Gap?

You may be afraid that your gifts will be used on **unproven programs,** bloated overhead, or wasteful events; it's painful to think of resources being used this way when they could have done good elsewhere.

Perhaps you fear that your generosity will be **unrecognizable,** that you or anyone else will be unable to tie your particular gift to the change it brought about, and your personal sense of gratification will be lost.

Are you afraid of being **trapped?** You may think that if you give now, they'll ask for more later and never stop asking. The stress of constantly deciding whether to say yes or no without a strong vision to guide your choices can be discouraging.

The thought of **other people suffering** because your giving fell short may also be something you fear. Perhaps you worry that your gift will not be significant enough, or that you won't have the time or skill to direct your resources to the most effective organization.

> Because of our human limits, we cannot always know the impact of our giving.

### What Will Move You Past the Gratification Gap?

First, I want to acknowledge that, because of our human limits, we cannot always know the impact of our giving. Generosity requires a certain amount of faith when we send our gifts into the world in response to God's call. My friend Mike Hogan shared with me this part of a prayer by Bishop Ken Untener that speaks to our wondering about effectiveness:

> We water seeds already planted, knowing that they hold future promise. We lay foundations that will need further development.
> We provide yeast that produces far beyond our capabilities.
> We cannot do everything, and there is a sense of liberation in realizing that.
> This enables us to do something, and to do it very well.
> It may be incomplete, but it is a beginning, a step along the way, an opportunity for the Lord's grace to enter and do the rest.
> We may never see the end results, but that is the difference between the master builder and the worker.

These words reassure us that there will naturally be a certain amount of mystery about the results of our generous work.

That said, for those stuck in the Gratification Gap, there is often still room to get more information and make more strategic decisions in order to maximize measurable impact and personal satisfaction. Here are some truths that will help you move beyond wondering and questioning.

**You have permission to only support people, causes, and projects that match your heart's desire.**

As steward of your resources, you have the freedom to decide where to direct those resources. The best guidance for making those decisions will come from your heart—the headline issues you react to emotionally, the personal struggles that have affected you, the moments when you encounter others in need, and the still small voice of God that speaks to you. You may not be used to giving from your heart because of all the other external demands and limits placed on you. But once you do, you'll find it gets easier and more natural.

> Knowing your heart lets you take a strong stance and say yes or no from a place of confidence and compassion.

Giving from your heart's desire is not selfish—those tender places have been given to you for a reason, to provoke you to action and deep engagement. Knowing your heart lets you take a strong stance and say yes or no from a place of confidence and compassion.

**You can find organizations that are effective.**

Once you've listened to your heart about your desires to change the world, you can engage your head in choosing the best way to make that change happen. You can start conversations with your spouse, friends, and clergy about your giving, research nonprofits that are doing work you admire, and engage a professional to guide your evaluation and giving strategy. These efforts take more time than giving only in response to requests, but they also greatly increase your sense of gratification.

## Steps out of the Gratification Gap

*1. Get more involved.*

If you're feeling detached and in the dark about what's happening with the organizations you support, I encourage you to reach out. Read the annual report cover to cover, and then call the nonprofit director to ask follow-up questions. Visit the field office. Walk the neighborhood. Offer to volunteer using your strengths. Let your feet follow your money.

When Mike Klonne found himself wondering about his effectiveness as a mentor, he looked to the larger issue of education and got deeply involved in improving inner city schools. "When you start to volunteer, if you believe in it and gain satisfaction from doing good things, it becomes contagious and builds momentum," Mike says. "Almost no problem is independent, so that leads you into peripheral problems." Eventually Mike helped start a school, Right Step Academy, in downtown Milwaukee, and he serves on their board of directors.

There are costs to getting more involved. "The deeper you get," Mike says, "the more you have to deal with stuff that isn't pretty. It's easier to volunteer 10 hours and help rebuild some things, mentor a child. When your commitment gets stronger, you have to deal with things that aren't simple or easy—political issues, other people who don't share your beliefs, the darker side of the reality of our world. You have to deal with frustrating bureaucracy. But I get a great feeling of personal satisfaction from being the change I want to see, to quote Gandhi."

### 2. Give to fewer organizations.

The solution to being spread too thin is to narrow your focus so that you can go deeper. How many nonprofits do you donate to every year? What if you cut that number in half? What if you

> Trust that your resources will do more good, for you and others, when they are concentrated.

spent all your volunteer time with one or two agencies? Paring down like this takes courage. You may wonder what people will think or worry about how they will replace your funds or efforts. But trust that your resources will do more good, for you and others, when they are concentrated. Using the Generosity Gameplan process will help you make these winnowing decisions with clarity and confidence.

### 3. Create a portfolio of giving.

I encourage clients to think of their charitable giving and volunteering as a portfolio they need to balance and diversify, similar to a financial portfolio. You can look at the range of sectors—social, financial, political, environmental, educational, medical, religious, and cultural—and check in with your heart as to which areas you want to be active in. Some of your headline issues may overlap, allowing you to address more than one sector through one organization.

In your portfolio, you will probably have charities that just have to receive your support because of your position in your family or your community. But once your heart's desire is clear and you are focused, the heart-led part of your portfolio will hold the most significance. Think of the Pareto principle of 80/20. Spend 80 percent of your currencies on the 20 percent of organizations and issues that are most important to you, and 20 percent on the remainder.

### 4. Clarify the results you want to see.

*Ready, fire, aim* might work in some parts of your life, but when it comes to getting out of the Gratification Gap, I wouldn't depend on it. If you don't know what you're aiming for, you won't know when you've hit the mark. Get specific about the qualitative and quantitative goals that you are pursuing through your giving. Find out how nonprofits measure their effectiveness and track it.

Frank Hanna believes that many of us in philanthropic work are now seeking, not just incremental change, but a change of paradigms—we hope for revolutionary, dramatic improvements in the welfare of people and planet. But he cautions, "Even as we seek such change, the fact that we may not observe it doesn't mean that good isn't happening. 99.9 percent of all doctors don't do anything that changes the medical paradigm, but they still heal people. Paradigm change is a good thing to work for, but it's rare. It's what I spend my time on, but I don't know that everyone is equally called to that sort of thinking."

Thoughtful reflection and intentional relationships will bring the clarity and confidence you need. Know your heart's desire to create change, focus on that, and your generosity will be much more powerful.

> Thoughtful reflection and intentional relationships will bring the clarity and confidence you need.

# Study in Generosity: Julia Bolz

*While writing this book, I collected stories and thoughts from friends, clients, and colleagues on the subject of generosity. Several of them had lives that stood out as remarkable studies in the power of strategic giving. I wanted to share their personal stories with you in more detail to show what's possible when you give from your heart's desire to connect for good.*

The first Study in Generosity follows Julia Bolz from her law firm in Seattle to the war zone of the Middle East to the halls of Congress. I know Julia through her parents, Jack and Marian Bolz, who were on the board at Camp Manito-wish. Jack, Marian, and I have a friendship based on a common longing for thriving kids, faith, and family. I'm not surprised that they raised a daughter who became a rock star building schools in Afghanistan.

Jack used to bring a young Julia along with him to the nursing homes where he volunteered every week—they would play the piano together, and Jack would read to folks and serve them communion. Julia watched Marian working out in the community too as a big supporter of the arts and a firm believer in the link between music and healthy childhood development. Jack and Marian encouraged all their kids to find their own passion for volunteering, and Julia herself tried dozens of things until she slowly came to a focus on social justice work.

Julia became an international lawyer and a partner at a well-respected law firm in Seattle. Focusing on business immigration, she served as president of the Washington State Chapter of the American Immigration Lawyers Association. In those days, success for Julia was defined by good grades, a good salary, and a good job title.

## Emerging from the Action Gap

In the early 1990s, Julia's life turned on its head when her sister was diagnosed with ovarian cancer. While supporting her sister's recovery, she began questioning everything: "Do I like who I am? Do I like what I'm doing? Do I like the legacy that I'm going to leave behind?" She looked at this Julia the lawyer whom she had spent years creating, a person who billed in six-minute increments, and realized that she did not particularly like who she had become, where she was going, or how her values had shifted over time.

While soul-searching, Julia started asking herself new, audacious questions: "If I only had six months to live, what would I change? What kind of legacy do I want to leave behind?" Her heart led her to Africa, where she spent two years volunteering for various nongovernmental organizations (NGOs) all over the continent. As she experienced living in mud huts without running water or electricity and in townships built from tin sheds and cardboard boxes, Julia's life was transformed. The people she met in these places helped her see that success wasn't about how much money you earned or the titles you held; it was about the quality of your relationships and giving back to the people around you.

> As she experienced living in mud huts without running water or electricity and in townships built from tin sheds and cardboard boxes, Julia's life was transformed.

Subsequently, Julia resigned from her law partnership to serve as a social justice activist and human rights lawyer in the developing world. Along the way, she did every kind of volunteer work imaginable, from helping to amend constitutions to supporting microfinance organizations. Then, after the travesty of September 11, 2001, Julia felt a calling to go to Afghanistan. "I was one of the first development workers to go into the war zone," she says. "My desire was to work with Afghan women and children who at the time were clearly the most poor and oppressed in the world."

What she saw in Afghanistan broke her heart. At that dark moment in time, after 30 years of devastating war, many Afghans were starving and homeless, living on less than a dollar a day. The Taliban had just been ousted from power, but for years the country's women had not been allowed to work or go to school or even leave their homes without a male escort. Covered from head to foot in burkas, women had their voices literally silenced.

Julia worked with a team of international development workers who spoke local languages and had developed relationships with the Afghans. Together they began talking with community leaders—everyone from government to religious officials—and asking them, "What do your communities need?" Time and again, they got the same response: "Build us schools."

Afghan kids going to school for the first time—this image imprinted itself on Julia's heart, but she was struck by the scale of the task at hand. In the villages she had visited, it wasn't just school buildings that were needed. Everything had been destroyed by the wars; there were no teachers, no pencils, and no books.

## Building Connections

Back in Seattle in the spring of 2002, Julia began visiting schools and talking to kids about what she had seen and experienced in Afghanistan. One neighborhood school Julia visited had burned to the ground a few months earlier. "Here I was at their makeshift school," she says, "and I went in and gave one of my show-and-tell presentations, dressing the students up in Afghan clothes, talking with them about life on $1 per day, and showing them pictures of kids attending school in a dirt field. And these kids who had just lost a school said, 'We want to help you build a school for kids who never had one.'" The students ended up raising $4,000 through bake sales, concerts, and even by donating their own babysitting money. The money was combined with other contributions, which added up to $30,000 altogether. With that shoestring budget in 2003, in a village in northern Afghanistan, one of the first schools for Afghan girls was built. On the first day, more than 400 girls of all ages and multiple ethnic groups showed up for classes.

"One of my strengths," Julia says, "is that I'm as comfortable in a mud hut in a village as I am in the halls of Congress, which is unusual." She saw people with good intentions working for big aid agencies stuck behind barbed wire and tanks, unwilling or unable to leave their buildings. By living in the communities, sharing meals, helping people solve their problems, and celebrating with them, she was better able to share their stories with those in a position to help. Her connections made her a more effective advocate.

> Her connections made her a more effective advocate.

Her experience helped her to see that building relationships with all community stakeholders and empowering them to create peaceful, just, and sustainable solutions was like building a solid foundation under a house. She saw well-intentioned projects fail and schools built by other organizations burnt down or blown up. Julia began to understand what the missing ingredient was for a lot of these projects—a sense of community ownership—and decided to adopt a philosophy of partnership. The most effective way to help people, it seemed, was to offer them a hand up instead of a hand out. She could provide bricks and mortar and call it a day, but a school was more than just these material things, it was the community that would provide teachers and the labor to build the school and support it by sending their kids to learn.

Partnership was also about accountability, so sometimes Julia had to play the role of bad cop. In one situation, in the midst of building a school, the men in the community stopped coming to work. Julia sent out a notice issuing an ultimatum—unless the men returned to work the next day and lived up to their side of the bargain, she would simply move to another community that needed a school. She needed to convey how serious she was about the project and hold them accountable for being serious about it too. The next day, there were 50 men at the site, including the mayor and the imam, armed with shovels and ready to pitch in to get the school built.

Eventually, with the support of her international teammates who lived full time in Afghanistan, Julia eventually raised funds to build or repair 40 schools in Balkh Province in north-central Afghanistan, serving approximately 25,000 boys and girls and impacting 175,000 family members. Equipped with such things as libraries, computer centers, science labs, and teacher training facilities, the schools still stand today, attesting to the success of Julia's philosophy and work.

An organization called Ayni Education International was born from Julia's efforts. The word ayni is a worldview and way of life that comes from the Peruvian Andes and means "sacred reciprocity." Grasping the concept of *ayni* was one of Julia's deepest lessons from time she spent in Afghanistan, the principle that helped her evolve a transformational generosity. As she describes it, "Ayni is the interchange of loving-kindness, knowledge, and fruits of one's labor between individuals, the environment, and

Spirit. It is a foundation for ensuring the flow of love within oneself, within one's community, and in the greater world. To ensure the flow of *ayni* (whether within oneself or a community), giving and receiving must come from a place of true love. And, the flow must go both ways. For example, if I just give money or resources to you, I will eventually get tired and go away. Alternatively, if I simply receive from you, I will get lethargic and may stop working altogether."

Consequently, Julia worked not only to teach the Afghans and help them build peaceful, just, and life-affirming communities but to learn from them and build peace and bridges of understanding between their countries. To this end, she spoke over 500 times across America and advocated for education in the developing world with everyone from members of Congress, the White House, and State Department to civic and religious organizations, students, the U.S. military, and nonprofits like Rotary and National Geographic. By the time she stepped away from Ayni Education International at the end of 2011, some 50,000 people from across the country had supported her efforts in one way or another. Eventually, her passion and conviction won over folks who initially disagreed with what she was doing—people hurt by the tragedy of 9/11 who felt she was helping the enemy.

## Transformed by Generosity

While studying *ayni*, Julia learned that, "At a community level, ayni means working together as a group for the group; sharing resources and ideas; serving another out of kindness and compassion, knowing you may never be repaid directly, but understanding you'll always be provided for in the future; spending time together and celebrating the gifts of life; and having a sense of responsibility, not just for now but in the future. This requires one to be vulnerable, trustworthy, nonjudgmental, and open to giving love as well as receiving it."

In the 10 years Julia spent working between communities in Afghanistan and America, she began to notice that ayni was not flowing smoothly in her or through her at times: she was good at giving, for example, but she struggled with the backward flow of generosity. While she was able to make what seemed impossible possible through her sheer dedication and effort, Julia found it difficult to open up her arms to receive. "I also slowly recognized that a lot of the motivation that went into building the schools didn't come from a place of true love, respect, or kindness, but from fears, hurts and wounds. In looking back, I could see that one school was built out of a need to please or a need to be seen and another out of duty and obligation." Underneath this, Julia discovered she was carrying a deep, heavy guilt for having access to so much while so many people were hungry, cold, and suffering.

Thus, with the help of colleagues, Julia intentionally began to clear away the cobwebs of negative energies, patterns, and stories keeping her from fully stepping into her authentic, divine self, and she slowly but surely started to transform from the inside out. She saw that giving from a place of obligation completely changed the dynamic of the interaction, and so she practiced giving from a place of love rather than guilt. "In making this transition, I saw that I could no longer view others as 'poor,' because if they're

> The quality of Julia's philanthropy began to transform and she stopped feeling a hunger to please God. Instead, she allowed God's love to flow through her and become the force behind her charity (love in action).

poor, then they're victims. Instead, we are all connected, all one, and all equal in God's eyes." The quality of Julia's philanthropy began to transform and she stopped feeling a hunger to please God. Instead, she allowed God's love to flow through her and become the force behind her charity (love in action).

As impossible as it sounds, Julia learned to forgive the militants who had killed or kidnapped her friends in Afghanistan. She built relationships with warlords and those who hated the West, non-Muslims, and women. She helped build coalitions between people who at one time were intent on killing each other. Even though she was still working in a warzone, Julia began to feel a deep sense of peace, harmony, and balance.

On the last of 16 trips to Afghanistan over the course of a decade, Julia attended the dedication of a new $300,000 school for 3,000 girls. For the first time, instead of feeling an urgency to attend to the next task, she let herself enjoy the moment, relax into the satisfaction of a job well done, and accept the heart-felt gratitude of the Afghans. That was a brand new experience for her.

# Part II: A Fresh Playbook for Generosity

Jim and Lauren are intrigued by the possibilities of transformational generosity. They see the potential for getting more engaged in their giving.

When the girls were in middle and high school, Lauren was in the Action Gap, often saying, "When the girls are out of high school, I'll have more time to be generous." She channeled all of her energy into activities and causes that mirrored the girls' lives.

Lauren's appreciation for the importance of the arts became a heart issue when two of her daughters thrived on dance and music. She saw them become whole through their artistic expression and always wished that she had developed this side of herself, growing up. Her third daughter was the compassionate one, always connecting with the youth group at church and going on mission trips to serve others in distant places. As Lauren went along to chaperone, she could not help but get caught up in the needs of the poor in the developing world.

Now that Jim and Lauren's kids are out of the house, they're looking for something meaningful to do together, and these experiences with her daughters are informing Lauren's Generosity Gameplan.

In Part II, we'll explore how Jim and Lauren can approach generosity from a new perspective, involving their whole selves in charitable giving and volunteering.

Chapter 7

# Re-imagining Generosity

Are you ready to do generosity differently?

Do you want to take your giving to the next level with deep engagement and effectiveness?

In this book we are re-imagining what generosity looks like and feels like. So far we've explored some of the problems—the Generosity Gaps that appear when we practice transactional giving, which looks like an exchange and can feel detached and unfulfilling. Now it's time to dig in to transformational generosity, which looks like a relationship and feels alive and satisfying.

## What Does Generosity Mean?

As you would expect, I have lots of conversations with my friends and clients about charitable giving and volunteering. And I've discovered that some of them don't care for the word generosity.

Mike Klonne, who I mentioned in the last chapter, says that *generosity* isn't a word he would attach to what he does. He feels that it's a "first-person" word that puts the emphasis on the doer or the giver rather than the mission to create change. Mike says, "I would personally describe my volunteering and helping as a blessing given to me that I have been fortunate enough to realize." I appreciate Mike's gratitude and outward focus in what he does.

> "Me, generous? No, this is just what I do. It's the way I am. I don't consider it generous."

Some folks say, "Me, generous? No, this is just what I do. It's the way I am. I don't consider it generous." They somehow connect being generous with sacrificing, doing without, and having less that they had before. Indeed, behaving sacrificially and doing without is a healthy posture, but it's not the only posture of generosity. In fact, when sacrifice is the only picture of success, the Generosity Gaps grow larger.

My friends Harville Hendrix and Helen LaKelly Hunt are a couple who have served together for many years teaching their Imago Relationship Therapy in support of marriages all over the world. Helen is also a major donor and co-founder of Women Moving Millions, a global funding initiative encouraging women to make unprecedented gifts of $1 million or more for the advancement of girls and women. So they know whereof they speak!

"I never thought of myself as generous," Harville says. "I was just called to service, first as a social helper and then as a therapist. Generosity has a certain top-down quality: I'm the one giving to you and you're the needy one."

"I don't like the word *charity* either," says Helen. "The etymology has to do with opening the heart, which is good, but I think charity can be held suspect because it is seen as separate from real work, from the real world. I think it is wise to apply a business lens, to take generosity as seriously as strategic thinking and corporate development. The word generosity makes it sound like a luxury, like an option. But it's essential that we live generously."

> "...the return on social investment is that you live in a different and better world."

Harville and Helen like to think of giving and volunteering as a social investment. There's an egalitarian sense to the word; everyone gets to be a giver.

Investing is always done in anticipation of a return. "But the return on social investment is that you live in a different and better world," says Harville. "The return is not in kind but in quality of being."

"Investing is dynamic," adds Helen. "Everyone gets to be generous. If you give, that gift gets amplified, and there's an unleashing of the heart. Instead of you being the only one expressing your generosity, one person's heart opens others."

I can understand the discomfort with the word *generosity* and its connotation of superiority and selflessness, and I like very much the vision of social investing that Helen and Harville describe. Still, I find myself drawn to the rich linguistic origins of generosity as well as its spiritual resonance.

My friend and Ignatian companion, Dr. Paul Schervish of Boston College, says that the Latin roots of the word speak of *genus*, meaning the community of common origin, and *osus* or *osity*, meaning fullness and abundance. These two roots come together to form an expression of being fully engaged in life by being fully connected to the community. If we look at humanity as our shared origin, generosity is grounded in meaningful relationships, beginning with those inherited at birth through family, to our neighbors and playmates as children, to our classmates, colleagues, and other companions discovered throughout our lifetimes.

Relationships form the very crux of transformational generosity—we must leave behind the notion of generosity as an act of giving whose material reward is solely the receivers', while the givers must figure out how to continue being generous with fewer resources than they had before. In Harville's words, all who participate in generosity receive a return in quality of being. Generosity rooted in relationship becomes a posture toward others that stands on a foundation of love, motivating us toward curiosity rather than judgment and empathy over pity, not only toward those with whom we have existing connections, but also to each member of our shared humanity.

## Starting with a Disposition of Gratitude

*"A person must get connected with how he or she has received love and generosity. If you can't receive generosity, you can't receive grace. Without this connection, this self-awareness, one can only act generous, and generosity becomes a utility. What have you been given?"* Dr. Harville Hendrix

So how do we embark on this practice of transformational generosity driven by connection? We start with a disposition of gratitude. We are recipients of generosity from the moment we are born with the gift of life, loved and cared for. Through no effort of our own, we have marvelous bodies, intriguing personalities, and useful strengths. We are blessed by material comforts and the beauty of the natural world.

Micah and I were at a father-son banquet at Marquette University High School when we heard this story from Charlie Plumb, a former Navy fighter pilot and prisoner of war. Here's how he tells it in his book, *Insights Into Excellence:*

Recently, I was sitting in a restaurant in Kansas City. A man about two tables away kept looking at me. I didn't recognize him. A few minutes into our meal he stood up and walked over to my table, looked down at me, pointed his finger in my face and said, "You're Captain Plumb."

I looked up and I said, "Yes sir, I'm Captain Plumb."

He said, "You flew jet fighters in Vietnam. You were on the aircraft carrier Kitty Hawk. You were shot down.

You parachuted into enemy hands and spent six years as
a prisoner of war."

I said, "How in the world did you know all that?"

He replied, "Because I packed your parachute."

I was speechless. I staggered to my feet and held out a
very grateful hand of thanks. This guy came up with just
the proper words. He grabbed my hand, he pumped my
arm and said, "I guess it worked."

The young men and dads who heard this story at the banquet
were stunned by the breathtakingly ordinary duty and nearly invisible act that man performed for Captain Plumb. We are all
wearing virtual parachutes—privileges, benefits, and safety nets
that have been given to us through no personal merit.

Dr. Schervish says that there
are three ways to receive a gift:
you can take it with gratitude,
take it for granted, or take it with
guilt. Taking things for granted
leaves us disconnected, as though
the gift were never given. Taking
things with guilt is debilitating,
an expression of unworthiness
where the gift creates obligation. "When gifts are taken with
gratitude, they are understood to have been given freely, and that
does something to the heart," Dr. Schervish says. "We are led to
move forward with our vocation. Gratitude creates awareness of
having received care, and once that's learned, we can then give
care more abundantly."

> There are three
> ways to receive a
> gift: you can take it
> with gratitude, take
> it for granted, or
> take it with guilt.

The disposition of gratitude that Dr. Schervish describes
moves us beyond giving from the reciprocity motive. With no
tinge of guilt, we can give purely because we are meant to, be-

cause our hearts are open, because there is no sense of obligation, but instead great freedom.

The fresh playbook for generosity that I am laying out in this book has three fundamentals:

- Giving from your **heart's desire** for connection.

- Giving your **renewable currencies** of relationships, strengths, and resources.

- Giving in a way that makes use of the **multiplier effect.**

Let's begin in the next chapter by exploring your heart's desire and how it can change the way you give.

# Chapter 8

# Your Heart's Desire

*"When generosity is your heart's desire—when your heart is in it—you're following your deepest longings to change the world."*
Monsignor Don Fischer

When I talk about giving from your heart's desire, I mean two things:

- Your desire for **connection**: For a sense of interdependence and belonging, for company and conversation, to know that you are loved and loving.

- Your passion for creating a **certain kind of change:** Your compassion for a particular group of people or an aspect of the planet that results from your personal connections.

In this chapter I will focus more on the first idea—that we were created to be in relationship with God, our true selves, and others. When we get to the Generosity Gameplan process, I'll talk more about how those relationships provide strategic guidance for your giving.

**I believe that humans are hardwired for connection. We are happier and healthier and the world is a better place when we operate as part of a community.**

Quite fittingly, that belief comes from my connection to other people—from lived experience, communal wisdom, and spiritual teaching. As I share my ideas about practicing generosity from our heart's desire, I do so with a disposition of gratitude for the impact of mentors, friends, and family who have helped me bring these ideas together.

My understanding of the heart's desire and its influence on generosity comes from three main sources: *spirituality, biology, and sociology*. I'm sure we could find insights about the heart in almost every area of human study, but these are the three that have impressed themselves on me, in great part because of the people behind them.

## The Spirituality of the Heart

The man I first met as Father Don Fischer, my parish youth pastor when I was a teenager, has now become Monsignor Don Fischer. He is retired from active ministry but still serves with the Pastoral Reflections Institute he founded, hosting a radio show/podcast, and leading in-person pilgrimages in Tuscany.

Monsignor Don has remained my friend and mentor over the years, and in preparation for this book, he and I had a daylong conversation at his home in East Dallas. He opened up his understanding of generosity, beginning with the great commandment to "love the Lord, your God, with all your heart, with all your soul, and with all your mind" (Matthew 22:37).

> We all have an authentic longing to create real change and bring life to people—to nurture, relate, and transform.

Don reminded me that we were taught that this meant to "love God a lot." But, he suggested, what if loving with our heart meant connecting with God? And what if connecting with God meant simply connecting with our true selves, acting on the way God designed us . . . for relationship, not isolation? We all have an authentic longing to create real change and bring life to people—to nurture, relate, and transform.

"I usually think of money when I think of generosity," he said, "and there are two postures I see. *You should be giving money*, because if you're not, you're a bad person. You've got too much. You've got to share it. The other posture is *you'll feel better if you give your money away.* In my experience, both postures seem to bring on isolation. This isolation comes from feelings of shame about who you are or guilt about not giving enough. John, you're talking about developing community around one's generosity so that spirit and relationship interact. These are matters of the heart, not the head."

### Isolation is the Enemy of Generosity

The story of Adam and Eve is all about isolation. Two people are seduced by spiritual resistance, by the culture of power and autonomy. The culture's voice says, "We can do anything except one thing—we can't eat of the tree of the Knowledge of Good and Evil." So what's that?

That is you becoming the determiner, the knowledge, the rule-maker. You decide that "This is the way my life is going to work, and I choose it because it's mine—to get as much as I can get, to be in charge of everything, to control things." We're all susceptible to that. That's one way to live life that makes us feel good.

But when you chose to be autonomous of God, you're choosing to be autonomous of yourself. You have a nature that is designed by God to be your true self in the world. Author and social entrepreneur Bob Buford likes to say that one of the two "final exam" questions asked by our Maker will be, "Why weren't you more like you?"

So, what do I love about God's response to Adam and Eve? The character who gets the biggest punishment is the serpent; he is isolated, thrown out of the garden to forever crawl on his belly. Adam and Eve get the struggle that their choice creates for them—toil, work, difficulty, and sweat. The woman is going to be in pain over childbirth, which has a literal meaning, but in the context of generosity means giving birth to things is going to be both difficult and marvelous. Over thousands of years since Adam and Eve, God has tried to get us to see that we are hard-wired to be connected to our true selves and to God—working, learning, and celebrating together. This is a disposition of humility and dependence on God in terms of who you are. If I have an image of John Stanley that is different from my heart's longing and more than God intended me to be, I'm going to live with tension.

**Your true self, then, is a reflection of God, the facet of God you're asked to bring to the world.** I want to give you a way of being in the world that invites you to live in response to everything that makes you unique: your relationships, strengths, and resources.

The day I spent with Don happened shortly after my stepdad of 46 years, Ed Toogood, died, so stories of the heart were really resonating. During Dad's final days, our family was occupied with matters of the head and the heart: "What's going on in his body?" "Can he be fixed?" and "We might lose him." One of his good friends, who I had never met, caught me after daily mass and asked how he was doing. I wondered out loud whether it was congestive heart failure or cancer that caused his labored breathing. It turned out that Richard Woods, Dad's friend, was a recently retired cardiac surgeon who had been a pioneer in heart transplants. *Are you kidding?* I thought. *Right here when my family and I are at wit's end and need an advisor, you just show up in our lives?* Dr. Woods spent the entire morning with us, and many days afterward, not doctoring but being fully present to us with his heart and head, informing us and giving us confidence about Dad's future, regardless of outcomes. He delivered a profound act of generosity where no resources were transferred, just presence. We needed what only Richard Woods could give.

So, what happens when two or more come together around a need and put their hearts into it? If world-changing is the agenda, other strengths cascade forward, along with relationships and resources. You give all you've got and never miss what you give away.

> You give all you've got and never miss what you give away.

## The Biology of the Heart

Beneath the New Mexico peaks that inspired Georgia O'Keefe's paintings, Jamee and I had the privilege of gathering in conversation with twelve of the world's best relationship experts. Our role? Co-laborers to launch what was to become Relationships First, an initiative to awaken the world, especially couples, to the importance of lifelong healthy relationships. The conversation was way beyond my bachelor's degree and out of my practical nature, but it fit with my sense of adventure to make no small plans.

Among the experts in the room was Dr. Dan Siegel, who received his medical degree from Harvard University and completed his postgraduate medical education at UCLA with training in pediatrics and child, adolescent, and adult psychiatry. One of Dan's roles in the group was to bring to life his newly published book, *Mindsight*, in which he revealed discoveries in interpersonal neurobiology, combining many sciences into one perspective. I summarize it this way: first, when you know

> In the end, what we pay the most attention to defines us. How you choose to spend the irreplaceable hours of your life literally transforms you.

how the brain works, you can change the way it works; and second, learning happens in relationship. Dan is an elegant and effective teacher. As he says on his website, DrDanSiegel.com, he and his wife, Caroline, are working hard "to bring more kindness, compassion, and resilience into our world."

Relationships First co-laborer Diane Ackerman, a poet, essayist, and naturalist, and the author of *The Zookeeper's Wife* and *A Natural History of the Senses,* describes the new science this way: "A relatively new field, called interpersonal neurobiology, draws its vigor from one of the great discoveries of our era: that the brain is constantly rewiring itself based on daily life. In the end, what we pay the most attention to defines us. How you choose to spend the irreplaceable hours of your life literally transforms you."[16] If you choose to be intentional about your generosity, you *will* be changed, even down to the biological level.

Our brain development process begins very early in life and is rooted in relationship. As Dan writes in *Mindsight,* "We come into the world wired to make connections with one another, and the subsequent neural shaping of our brain, the very foundation of our sense of self, is built upon these intimate exchanges between the infant and her caregivers. In the early years this interpersonal regulation is essential for survival, but throughout our lives we continue to need such connections for a sense of vitality and well-being." How fascinating that there is a neurological imperative for connection, not just a moral or social one.

And there is a place for the heart in all of this too. Dan writes, "The networks of nerve cells around the heart and throughout the body communicate directly with the social parts of our brain and they send that heartfelt sense right up to our prefrontal areas." The heart contributes to our intuition, giving us access to the wisdom of our body by sending information to the brain that draws on our passions, our "heartfelt sense" of what to do.

So the brain feeds on the intuitive signals sent by our hearts, and it also depends on the relationships that are formed out of love and a desire for communion. As Dan describes so beautifully, "Such joining happens when we attune to the internal shifts in another person, as they attune to us, and our two worlds become linked as one. Through facial expressions and tones of voice, gestures and postures—we come to 'resonate' with one another. The whole we create together is truly larger than our individual identities. We feel this resonance as a palpable sense of connection and aliveness. This is what happens when our minds meet." And this vision is what I'm working toward, that this resonance would be present in every meeting and phone call in the philanthropic world.

Dan teaches that, whether you are considering mental health, physiological health, or longevity, the most important factor in all studies of personal well-being is relationships. Isolation erodes well-being, and relationships born out of intentional reflection produce resilience in whatever we take on in our generous lives.

> Where you focus your attention and how you focus your mind can actually change the structure of the brain, resulting in changed behavior, attitudes, and outcomes.

Perhaps you've heard of the studies Dan talks about, where people are given $20 and then asked to spend it on themselves or give it away. When they give the $20 away, reward circuits driven by dopamine activate in their brains, resulting in feelings of well-being. When we are generous with others, we are happier ourselves.

So can interpersonal neurobiology help us take generosity to the next level? Can old dogs learn new tricks? Yes, indeed.

Where you focus your attention and how you focus your mind can actually change the structure of the brain, resulting in changed behavior, attitudes, and outcomes. Developing your reflective abilities, for instance, allows you to connect with your own feelings and sensibilities, which are the basis for social intelligence. What social intelligence? The pressing need for empathy, kindness, and compassion toward others, for example.

This is what especially excites me about Dan's message, that at any age we can improve our skills at what he calls *mindsight*: "this important ability that allows us to see and shape the inner workings of our own minds." The physical structures of our brains can change in positive ways, and these skills and changes lead to further well-being. The goal, Dan says, is *integration*: "a process by which separate elements are linked together into a working whole." The Generosity Gameplan process is one way to reflect on your experience and beliefs about generosity and integrate your philanthropic efforts with who you really are.

When two people begin with reflection and honor each other with care, an integrated relationship forms and results in stimulating growth of the integrated fibers of the brain. The result? Increased awareness of feelings, understanding, and intuition . . . a moral compass. Generosity.

## The Sociology of the Heart

*"The antidote to isolation and autonomy is to turn your connections into relationships by giving without expecting repayment."*
Dr. Harville Hendrix

Despite our best efforts at independence, "doing it my way," rugged American individualism, and movements that empower young adults to "grow up," there remains an innate longing for others. Some would even characterize it as a groaning for healthy relationship.

Sitting in his study in Abiquiú, New Mexico, looking out on the high desert, my good friend Harville Hendrix poured himself into me one day as we talked about the future of our adult kids, books, work, and generosity. He reminded me about philosopher Martin Buber, who suggests that some people go through life with an I-it posture. The other person becomes one to be positioned, manipulated, or used. This dishonors the other as a person and is a vertical relationship.

On the other hand, the I-Thou posture connects us to others horizontally as co-equals in life and work. The receiver is elevated to personhood. This is the posture that Harville and his partner, Helen LaKelly Hunt, live and promote in Imago Relationship Therapy, a worldwide association of relationship therapists that they imagined and developed. More than 2,000 therapists worldwide use their therapy models. Helen has also used this horizontal worldview in her stunning work to empower women's philanthropy through Women Moving Millions (over 180 women have each pledged at least $1 million).

As the afternoon turned to evening, Harville proposed that giving without expecting repayment is a paradox. It is counter to our society's focus on self. Our capitalistic system, for instance, both empowers generosity and stands in its way. It empowers it by offering access to opportunity and recognizing individual achievement, which in turn increases an individual's confidence. It stands in the way of generosity when self becomes more important than

> Generosity, rightly understood, is grounded in a growing interior life and in our most meaningful relationships.

other. If the culture supports it, people can stay isolated. In my fresh playbook for generosity, I propose that we choose to be other-centered.

At breakfast the next morning, before heading off to the airport, Harville, Helen, and I concluded that generosity, rightly understood, is grounded in a growing interior life and in our most meaningful relationships. Those relationships are characterized by their simple and powerful relationship fundamental, "moving from judgment to curiosity." Curiosity about another person opens the door to empathy. An empathic presence, being intentionally present in time, attention, and space, is powerful for both parties and leads to generosity.

## On Whom Will I Depend?

Frank Hanna is successful in business, and friends often seek him out after their adult sons graduate from college. "Will you visit with my son, Frank? He is just getting started and you are a good role model for him."

Frank is known to ask a shocker of a question when he meets these men in their early twenties. He listens to them speak for a while about their career plans, and then he asks, "Are you looking for someone to marry?"

You can see the strapping testosterone-filled young men squirming in their seats. "Well, no, Mr. Hanna, I've got to get independent first. I have to get established in my career, travel, and get some experience living on my own."

While this answer might sound great for parents whose sons have extended their adolescence far past college, Frank's faith-filled response might surprise you. "Independence? You've got to be kidding, son. Listen, God has been gracious to me, and I have had success at business and at life, but I am completely dependent on my wife of many years and the people with whom I work each day. I could do little without them. I like to say, 'I married the best person I know.' Most importantly, I start each day completely dependent on God. So you see, thriving independence is a myth." One of the first questions a young man or woman asks should not be "How independent can I become?" but "On whom will I depend?"

So, we have a capacity to resonate from our heart to someone else. This is why the world was created. This is what parents give their children. Science has shown that heart cells are stimulated when another beating heart is nearby, especially if the other person is intentional and compassionate. This kind of presence is what Harville calls empathic resonance, and it is given to you by God for the good of others. Everyone has this gift, but no one else's is the same. Your heart's desire for connection can make the world a better place.

Chapter 9

# Your Renewable Currencies

I used to think that loving with all my heart or putting my heart into something meant that I did it often or with great intensity. But as we saw in the last chapter, this is not so: loving with our hearts or putting our hearts into something is a conscious act of connecting. When you are following your deepest longing to change the world and your heart is engaged, that's where you'll spend yourself, and that's when transactional giving becomes transformational generosity.

Connecting your heart to another's awakens a capacity for presence—the uniqueness you bring to the world. My presence is my unique gift from God for the world. Everyone has this gift, and this gift is meant to be given away.

Your unique presence transforms the traditional currencies of time, talent, and treasure into **the renewable currencies of relationships, strengths, and resources.** When you spend these renewable currencies, instead of feeling like you have less after you donate or volunteer, you feel energized and replenished. Instead of being interchangeable with other donors and volunteers, you are irreplaceable and deeply valued for what you give.

> When you are following your deepest longing to change the world and your heart is engaged, that's where you'll spend yourself, and that's when transactional giving becomes transformational generosity.

The order of these renewable currencies is important. We must begin by giving to and through our relationships to ensure that our hearts are connecting before we consider giving service or money. The good news is that this order of giving increases our pleasure in giving and makes our decisions easier.

When generosity is an expression of who you are, rather than what you have, you can buckle your seat belt for personal transformation. The question becomes "How well do I share?" rather than "How much do I share?" You'll find it very liberating to *be generous* instead of *doing generosity.*

## Spending Your Relationships

*"When we honestly ask ourselves which person in our lives means the most to us, we often find that it is those who, instead of giving advice, solutions, or cures, have chosen rather to share our pain and touch our wounds with a warm and tender hand."* Henri Nouwen

Being generous with your relationships may not be the first thing that comes to mind when you think of philanthropy. The concept of relational equity or social capital is well known in the business world, but let me describe it in broader terms.

> The more we extend ourselves, the larger our account grows, the richer our relationships become, and the greater influence we have.

Whether or not we are aware of it, everyone possesses a relationship capital account. This capital is the goodwill that others have toward us. We spend this capital to get things done when we ask a favor, influence others to do something, or lead others in a project. We spend the capital in this account to avoid loneliness and to navigate our families, neighborhoods, workplaces, and communities.

The funny thing about this account is that we cannot make deposits to it directly—we must rely on others. And they make deposits when we extend ourselves to them without expecting repayment. The more we extend ourselves, the larger our account grows, the richer our relationships become, and the greater influence we have. Life becomes more joyful. Try as we might to manipulate our relationship capital, the results are always the same. "She only did this because she wants something from me." Expecting *quid pro quo* from a relationship won't get a deposit.

I truly believe that **great relationships are contests in generosity.** We should be challenging each other, competing to see who can do more for the other person, rather than trying to get away with doing as little as possible. These contests begin at home with our spouses, children, and parents; every time you help your mother fix a computer problem or bring your wife tea or loan your son the car, your relationship account grows. Every compliment and expression of thanks, every thoughtful question, every errand you do on someone's behalf contributes.

(My friend Scott Stanley reminds me that we want to keep contests in generosity in the realm of positive escalation, where the motive is heaping love on the other. Keeping score in order to get your fair share is a bad sign in relationships, and that's not the kind of competition I'm encouraging.)

I'm fascinated by the research of my friend Dr. Bradford Wilcox, Associate Professor of Sociology at the University of Virginia and Director of the National Marriage Project. He and Jeffery Dew at Utah State University have just conducted a study on generosity and marriage, and the results back up my idea that great relationships are contests in generosity. Reporting on the study, they say, "We found that for both husbands and wives, generosity—defined here as small acts of kindness, displays of respect and affection, and a willingness to forgive one's spouse their faults and failings—was positively associated with marital satisfaction and negatively associated with marital conflict and perceived divorce likelihood." To me that says that generosity is not just a desirable virtue in the abstract—it means stronger families and happier couples.

Contests in generosity also extend to relationships at work and church, and in the wider community. There are so many ways for us to "[give] good things to others freely and abundantly," as the Science of Generosity defines the word, before we ever pull out our wallet.

Jeff Dew shared with me that "Although we've only done preliminary analyses up to this point, we are finding that generosity within marriage is positively associated with generosity in the community. In other words, husbands and wives who report being more generous toward their spouses also report spending more time volunteering and report higher levels of charitable donations. We also examined whether spending time with one's family (another form of generosity) was associated with volunteerism and charitable donations. Parents—particularly fathers— who report spending more time with their children also reported higher levels of volunteering and charitable donations."

One of my favorite ways to spend my relationships is by **building bridges between others** for their benefit, not mine. I've developed more relationships and friendships over time than I can possibly cultivate. And among these people, many have at least one thing in common: similar life experiences, challenges and solutions that overlap, a set of talents, or connections that would be the last tumbler that falls into place to unlock an opportunity. I love looking through my address book, discovering people who would profit from an introduction to each other, and getting them connected.

In my network of Ignatian Associates, Brother Jim Holub, SJ, had been incubating an idea for some time. He was, as the great Jesuit leader Pedro Arupe taught, "a man for others." He was driven by a deep commitment to social justice and a radical giving of oneself to others. He knew that there were gang members eager to leave the gang life but who needed a pathway to be whole. Many were under-educated but creative, as he could see by the tagging (graffiti) left on walls in his neighborhood. Some had the potential for a solid work ethic if they received some guidance and direction.

Jim started an organization, Homeboyz Interactive, that taught gang members to build and maintain websites with HTML in the early days of programming. After a year of training and life cleanup (clearing debt and police records and repairing broken relationships), Jim would get the young men placed as interns in Midwest companies that were hungry for in-house web skills.

Expansion was on Jim's mind, and my friend John was looking for great inner-city job training ideas to fund with his new foundation.

"How much do you need, Brother Jim?" we asked.

"I need $1 million," he told us. "I have good prospects but I need friends to help us get moving."

After some discernment, John and his foundation board decided to be the first $250,000 and the last $250,000, leaving Jim only $500,000 to raise. Within weeks, John was in the Homeboyz office announcing his intentions personally. After the announcement, Jim left the room abruptly and was gone for a few minutes. When he returned and was asked if he was okay, he said, "Oh yes! I just had to call my mother—she has been praying for this for a long time."

Soon after, three tattooed, body-pierced young men walked in pushing a cart with a computer and screen on it. They proceeded to share with John what they were going to be doing as interns at Amoco Corporation in Chicago starting the next week.

When John left that day, I don't believe his feet were touching the floor.

Mission and service in the Ignatian way is seen not as an individualistic enterprise, but as work done in collaboration with others. So what happened here? A relational bridge was built between John and Brother Jim for their benefit, not mine. Win, win, win!

> "Doing good in the community comes back to you in business, but if you set out to do good for that reason, it doesn't work."

My friend Tom Beerntsen is someone I think of when it comes to spending relationships. After working for the YMCA in Iowa, South Dakota, and Minnesota, he returned to his hometown of Manitowoc, Wisconsin to take over the family candy business, Beerntsen's Confectionary, when his father became ill. He didn't have a lot of money to give, but he started using his fundraising knowledge for local organizations, chairing five capital campaigns in nine years. "I got to know all the business and industrial leaders. A group of us moved from charity to charity, and I had a ball doing that volunteer work," Tom says. The goodwill he generated returned to him as Beerntsen's Confectionary prospered. "Doing good in the community comes back to you in business, but if you set out to do good for that reason, it doesn't work," he says.

Now, years later, Tom has sold the business to return to the nonprofit sector. He's currently in Chicago, and he shared with me an amazingly ordinary story about how his generosity with relationships came back to him. "I have always tried to treat everyone with respect, both staff and donors. I take an interest in them and try to do what I can. I worked with a young lady named Lauren at the YMCA Heritage Group in Illinois, and we got along really well. But she and the rest of the development crew were dismissed after that organization merged with the YMCA of Metropolitan Chicago. That was tough, seeing my great department eliminated! After that, Lauren applied for a job at the Lurie Children's Hospital and used me as a reference. She got to the finals of that competition but was eliminated at the very end, so the hospital recommended her to the Wood Family Foundation, which was started by retired Cubs pitcher Kerry Wood and his wife. As Lauren's reference, I learned about the foundation and discovered that they didn't have an executive director. One thing led to another, and the Wood Foundation hired me."

This story is a great illustration of the serendipitous progression of generosity in relationship, how we give to each other in various ways over time without knowing the good effects that will manifest in the future. Spending our relationship currency results in some wonderful surprises!

## Spending Your Strengths

*"We can do no great things, only small things with great love."*
Blessed Mother Teresa of Calcutta

Let's be clear about one thing—whatever the size and breadth of your strengths inventory, everyone has the talent of being genuinely present to another person. Presence is the most impactful, least costly, and least expected human talent. We frequently undervalue presence, but it is where we should begin.

"John, your talents will develop in response to other human beings. Be present and keep relating." That is what Don Clifton, then chairman of the Gallup Organization, said to me while we sat on his deck one evening. He had just spent a week with 16 business leaders from across the country, teaching them to discover and lead with their strengths. Clifton pioneered this approach to leadership, and in 1995, it was transformative to the corporate culture and personally transformative for me.

Don's point was that people grow when they have a chance to use their talents—**a talent put to practice turns into a strength.** When people get a chance to do what they do well, they look and feel like naturals. This truth applies to the marketplace and to the context of our generosity. Claim your strengths, starting with presence, and spend them. You'll grow and others will too.

My friend Rose Sweet writes and speaks about restoring broken relationships, and she's the creator of The Catholic's *DIVORCE SURVIVAL* Guide. Rose says that when she remembers a person needs her more than just her time, she can offer her presence as a gift that's less like a necktie or fruitcake at Christmas and more like the shiny red Schwinn bicycle the person really wanted.

Rose told me this story about what it means to give her full presence: "A divorced woman called me to order my DVD series. I gave her a cheerful voice, the pat encouragement, took her information, said I'd pray for her, and hung up. It was close to dinner and I had much to do. Not a minute later, I heard a Voice in my heart say, 'Rose, you gave her a teensy little fruitcake! *Stop* what you're doing, call her back, and ask if she needs someone to talk to. Give her what she *really* needs right now. You.' Okay . . . sheesh! I called her back and apologized that I had maybe not been as sensitive to her as I could have been, and did she want to talk a little bit? (Yes, I added that 'little bit' part.) She started crying and thanked me. She'd had such a bad day, and she poured out her pain, and I really listened. No advice, no encouragement. Just listening and groaning with her. She was immensely thankful and I felt really good afterward."

Beyond presence, we all have other strengths to share in almost every context. I've done many camping trips during my years with the YMCA, and I love watching how people naturally gravitate to what they're good at. Paddlers compare notes on whether they're better in the bow or at the stern and pair up accordingly. A big strong guy portages a canoe, and a smaller woman steers expertly between rocks in shallow water. When you arrive at a campsite, everyone gets out and divides up duties: one gets firewood, one rigs up a tarp over the picnic table, and a few others erect the tents. There's always someone good at reading a map, someone else who's a fantastic cook, and someone who leads the singing when it gets dark. I wish it were always this easy to get people to serve from their strengths!

If you'd like some insight into what your strengths are (since it's sometimes hard to see your own), I can highly recommend the Clifton StrengthsFinder assessment, first developed by Don Clifton along with Tom Rath and scientists at Gallup. I was fortunate to be a member of the earliest phase of StrengthsFinder, and getting clarity about my strengths has influenced the way I lead, live, and give. Here are three of my top strengths, in the assessment's own words, which you can see played out in my Generosity Gameplan work:

- People strong in the **Futuristic** theme are inspired by the future and what could be. They inspire others with their visions of the future.

- People who are strong in the **Relator** theme enjoy close relationships with others. They find deep satisfaction in working hard with friends to achieve a goal.

- People strong in the **Strategic** theme create alternative ways to proceed. Faced with any given scenario, they can quickly spot the relevant patterns and issues.

As you can imagine, I feel great when I am inspiring others with my vision of connected and strategic generosity!

Rose Sweet has another story that illustrates how she spends her strengths in her relationship with her three teenaged stepsons. This is another one of those examples of amazingly ordinary generosity: "In the 1970s I used to be a controller for a chain of health food stores, and then for nearly 30 years I was a commercial real estate appraiser. I have a good grasp of income and expenses and can whip out a budget like nobody's business. One weekend I invested my time with the boys in teaching them to make their own plans and budgets; I could have done it for them, but I can't . . . not if I truly love them. When they got frustrated with all the forms and numbers and concepts and wanted to walk away, I donated my sense of humor to ease the money shock. I made a distribution of assets (maturity) when I refused to kill them even when I wanted to! I gave of my interior gifts until I was ready for a cocktail and a nap (not necessarily in that order). But this morning I know that I gave what is best for them and what nobody else could do as well because of my natural talents and my personal love for them. *That's* an unbeatable combination that is sometimes difficult but ultimately very satisfying. John's concept of being truly present and giving of self rather than, or in addition to, money involves the cross."

> It's better to step up and own your strengths, ask questions about others' needs, and look for overlap.

Spending strengths is an area where it's particularly important that you take the lead because fundraisers and organizers don't necessarily know what your strengths are—they just know what they need. If you show up, they'll have you meet that need. It's tempting to fill a hole just because you can, but if the work isn't suited to you, things may not go well in the long term. Instead, it's better to step up and own your strengths, ask questions about others' needs, and look for overlap.

## Spending Your Resources

*"Never measure your generosity by what you give, but rather by what you have left."* Bishop Fulton Sheen

Maybe you're wondering why I call this currency resources instead of treasure. The simple answer is that treasure implies money, and most people have more resources to give than just money. I don't mean to take away the importance of money in charitable giving, but I want you thinking about your resources in a larger sense. Your net worth is more than just cash: you have many other kinds of assets that you can use to do good. You also have influence over other people's resources that you may not have considered.

Once you have spent time building bridges, fostering relationships, and serving from your strengths, the places where you want to spend your resources come into focus. When you are *asked* for a donation, you may have very little context in which to make a decision, and feel like you're fumbling for a rationale as to why you should give. But

> Once you have spent time building bridges, fostering relationships, and serving from your strengths, the places where you want to spend your resources come into focus.

when you are proactive and looking for a cause or project to support, you turn your eyes first to the people and needs you know and care about, and you have much more information about what's needed and why.

In a later chapter, you'll read the story of Gordon Hartman, who has channeled his business strengths and funds into building awareness of and support for children with disabilities like his daughter, Morgan. This work may seem like an obvious choice for a father, but Gordon said no to many other opportunities before he said yes to families of children with disabilities. Guided by his relationships with his daughter, her friends, and their caregivers, he saw how he could use his skill as an entrepreneur and property developer, and his money naturally followed.

Think about what resources you might have in your back pocket other than cash: real estate and other property, business assets, cars and personal possessions, and investment holdings. I know more and more people who are creatively tapping their resources in order to do good. John and Barb Findley purchased a lake house outside of Milwaukee, a 3000-square-foot summer cottage that they donated as a pastors' retreat. A host couple lives onsite, and there are six rooms available for pastors and their spouses to come and recharge. "I don't think people understand the life pastors and their families lead," John says. "They are living in a glass house 24/7, doing a job for which they're seldom thanked and often critiqued." The retreat gives these couples a chance to get reacquainted with each other and with God. They get three meals a day, a beautiful property to enjoy, and much-needed rest.

Calvin Edwards told me about a client who is a commercial real estate investor. He felt convicted to support an international program in the Middle East, but because of the recession, his shopping centers had a much higher vacancy rate than usual, and his income had gone down substantially, at least for a while. Instead of tightening his fist and not giving, or liquidating his real estate assets, he borrowed against them and gave away the loan he received. Then he gradually repaid the loan over several years. In this way, he was able to leverage his assets at a critical time to give at a higher level.

Think also about the people you could recruit to put their resources behind an organization or project. Early in his business career, Tom Beerntsen invested more into his business and less into community projects, but the work he did chairing capital campaigns in Manitowoc encouraged his connections to participate in the projects.

I hope you're getting excited about how you might spend these renewable currencies—relationships, strengths, and resources—now that you've looked at them in a new light. There are so many great ways to be generous when we widen our concept of what we have to give.

# Chapter 10

# The Multiplier Effect

We talked in the last chapter about the three renewable currencies and how to spend them. Now I'd like to delve into what makes these currencies renewable. I call it the *multiplier effect*. You give something away and you receive as much or more back in return. You give but your supply isn't diminished. Your gifts benefit both you and others in a win-win scenario. **This multiplier effect is a hallmark of transformational generosity.**

I imagine that Jesus delighted in giving us a miraculous example of the multiplier effect when he fed the 5,000 with only a few loaves and fishes. And I have many other modern-day stories to share about how people's generous efforts are being amplified when they spend their relationships, strengths, and resources.

The multiplier effect works because it takes into account the spiritual side of the equation as well as the material. Not everything important in life can be seen and quantified—**much wealth is invisible and experienced rather than touched.** Ted Baehr, chairman of the Christian Film and Television Commission, knows this well. He shared with me this testimonial about the Commission's work in the media: "We give the $100,000 Epiphany Prize to movies and televisions programs with faith and values. Our giving has multiplied what we have. Not only are there more movies with faith and values (1 percent in 1985 and 57 percent in 2011), but relationships have multiplied, resources have multiplied, and all the time, energy, and talent we have has increased. Without the spiritual, there are never enough resources; with God, all things are possible. That does not mean 'name it and claim it.' Sometimes the return is quite different than material resources, but it does mean that we can trust Him to do what He promises."

Note that the multiplier effect works primarily when it is a consequence of generosity and not the sole aim. We need to be other-focused in our efforts and giving mainly because we want to connect. The return we get when our currencies are replenished is then a welcome bonus that sustains us and allows us to give more.

## Multiplying Your Relationships

When you tend your relationships with love and attention, they naturally grow in a variety of ways.

**Your current relationships are deeper and more satisfying.**

Listening carefully and helping where you can turns acquaintances into friends and friends into cherished loved ones. Formal exchanges become intimate conversations. In more places in your life, you feel seen, heard, and appreciated. When you model concern for others, they model the same for you.

Let me share a personal story about the importance of generosity in deepening relationships. I have a young man working with me on the Generosity Gameplan, Michael, who is a friend of my son, Micah. When the boys were in high school, our family went away over Christmas, and Mike, encouraged by his friends, used our garage door code (given to him by Micah months earlier for a legitimate purpose) to get into the house with a bunch of other teenagers. They hung out in our family home with a few of their girlfriends, having some beers, as hyper-social, curious, fun-loving yet under-the-legal-drinking-age teenagers are wont to do. The crew was unaware that we had arranged a house-sitter and that she would be returning home shortly.

When she did, the teens scattered, and phone calls ensued between Wisconsin and Texas as the house-sitter told me what happened and I contacted the boys' parents. I'm sure none of them had a great Christmas break that year, anticipating the moment when they would have to march over to my house and give a face-to-face apology.

Mike arrived with his mother, and both of them were profusely apologetic. I suppose we could have involved the Marquette University High School administration, even the police. But Jamee and I felt that looking into the eyes of these remorseful young men and hearing them admit their wrongdoing would be a powerful moment. They'd been through enough punishment by this point.

I said to Mike, "You made a mistake, you admitted it and apologized, and I believe you. Now, let's get back on the right track." Mike has told me that being present to him in that moment, offering forgiveness and reconciliation, was an amazing act of generosity and made a big impression on him.

Jamee and I went on chaperoning dances, attending sporting events, and supporting Micah and Mike as they worked toward finishing high school and going on to college and careers. Now, Mike helps me with technology and communications, and I'm glad that our relationship has developed into something very special from that pivotal moment one Christmas.

**You create new rewarding relationships, often outside your existing circle or comfort zone.**

When you give more strategically, led by your heart's desire, you will likely venture into communities you hadn't been invited to explore before. A diversity of relationships creates empathy, openness, and cross-pollination of ideas.

Kent and Linda Bergemann told me that, when their boys were young, they were involved in activities that paralleled what Mark and Michael were doing. Kent was a scoutmaster in Boy

Scouts, and Linda organized things at their school. But now they are stretching beyond those familiar contexts and asking themselves, "Who don't we know?" They went to Israel and realized they didn't know any Muslims, so they got involved in inter-religious dialogue, made some Muslim friends, and now have people they can reach out to break down barriers. Linda became a Big Sister to Monica, a 17-year-old Latina girl, which was a real eye-opener as she began to understand the life of an undocumented young immigrant.

**The connections among people in your network proliferate and strengthen your community.**

As you bring others together in generosity, the links between them cross and build like a spider's web. Likeminded people are drawn to each other and band together to accomplish more.

Helen LaKelly Hunt works with women in philanthropy partly because she gets joy from seeing women step into their voice and power. Hers is a family of means (her father discovered the East Texas oil field), but the money was traditionally controlled by men. She says, "In the culture at the time, I saw others mishandle a lot of money and get involved in speculation, and that didn't seem like a healthy stewardship of money. I thought, 'What if the women had taken that money and done something?' But it was unheard of in my family and in the culture. I've been involved to shift that cultural value, so that women have an equal voice in how money is allocated, so it reflects their value systems. That feels like justice to me. There was a time when there weren't many voices of women in positions of leadership. That is changing." Helen's world is better because of the connections she has helped forge between women in her philanthropic community.

**You have more capital in your relationship account.**

When you know that people have your back because they sense your care and connection, you can put yourself out there, confident that your friends will support you.

Micah's friend Mike is now volunteering with an organization called Ganga Ghar, which supports impoverished children in Nepal through education. He got involved through his friend Ojash Shrestha, who started Ganga Ghar after a trip home to Nepal for his wedding. Seeing a 12-year-old girl working as a servant in his parents' home, Ojash realized he wanted to do something for the children who didn't have the advantages of education that he had. Ganga Ghar's circle of connection has grown organically, starting with family and close friends of Ojash and expanding every time a new team member or sponsor came on to support the work. Everyone who joins has a personal reason for wanting to work with the Ganga Ghar team, and their commitment is high because their hearts are on the line.

From the early days sponsoring five children to go to school in 2009, Ganga Ghar has raised its sights to building a permanent school in Nepal. Ojash and the rest of his team knew that they needed strong support to undertake such a demanding project for a small organization. And they also trusted the strength of their network to give them the financial and emotional boost they needed. In the fall of 2012, Ganga Ghar ran an online fundraiser and brought in over $15,000 from 152 funders to pay for a group scouting trip to Nepal. The Ganga Ghar team members have all invested in their personal connections, and that relationship capital is there to draw on when they need it to pursue their passion for helping children in Nepal.

## Multiplying Your Strengths

When you serve using your strengths, there are several important payoffs.

**You feel exhilarated.**

Why does it matter how you feel when you're volunteering? Because your emotions provide fuel for your service as well as feedback that you are serving in the right capacity.

> You are looking for opportunities where your energy is spent on creating change rather than getting motivated to show up.

Spending your strengths doesn't necessarily mean that your task will be easy; on the contrary, the volunteer assignment might be quite challenging. But you are looking for opportunities where your energy is spent on creating change rather than getting motivated to show up. Look for opportunities where you end the volunteer assignment feeling triumphant and enthusiastic, even when you're tired.

The feeling of exhilaration comes not just in excelling at what you do, but in being seen and appreciated for who you really are. Kent Bergemann knows the chief academic officer of a university—they met through their children's school—and she says right out, "Don't ask me to bake cookies! But I can help with strategic planning." Not only is this woman using her gifts more effectively when she's planning instead of baking, people can also connect with her more genuinely because she is serving from her true self.

**You get even better at what you do.**

When you're doing work that calls on your strengths, they continue to develop, often by leaps and bounds, because your passion drives you forward. You find yourself reaching to new levels so you can meet the challenges ahead. And when you are at the top of your game, your volunteering is even more meaningful and has more impact.

Julia Bolz spent years honing her skills as an international corporate lawyer, many of which came into play when she started working in the developing world as a social justice activist and human rights lawyer. Having travelled to more than 70 countries and engaged in a variety of work with the environment, health care, land reform, and microfinance, she not only saw the big picture but understood what things were like on the ground. In Afghanistan after 9/11, she was able to network, organize, negotiate, and connect with people at many levels. Over the decade she worked there, Julia became a nationally-recognized advocate for global education, meeting regularly face-to-face with government, religious, and community leaders about the importance of educating kids in the developing world. Now on sabbatical, Julia is preparing for the next chapter in life—a chapter she wants to make even bigger and more impactful.

## Multiplying Your Resources

So how does the multiplier effect work with your resources? By leveraging your contributions, overlapping your efforts with others, and multiplying the value of what your resources can do on their own.

Offering the Generosity Gameplan process is one of the ways that I multiply my resources. My heart is moved when I see families struggling in conflict or breaking apart. I can do a certain amount of good to build healthy families and strong marriages by spending my own currencies directly, and I try to do that through my family's foundation and personal giving. But I can do even more good by helping people of means and substance who also care about families give more strategically so that their currencies are creating the maximum benefit.

When Calvin Edwards evaluates a nonprofit organization so that his clients have information and guidance for decision-making, he has found a way to make the value of that work go further. "Not only do we do the research necessary to advise the client," he says, "we also package that research in such a way that it has utility for the nonprofit we scrutinize. The client gets what he wants and needs, and we've created two collateral benefits. We've prepared a document that the nonprofit can share with other donors, and we've shown the nonprofit where it can strengthen and improve so it can be in better shape when the next donor comes along." Calvin says that they only share this information when they have their donor client's permission. "In almost every case, we get that permission, and the client is thrilled. It mitigates their concern that money going to the consultant is not going to the cause. This way the nonprofit gets a valuable in-kind gift."

Calvin told me another story about a client who had served as a faithful long-time board member for an organization but had decided that it was time to move on. He announced the departure diplomatically and told the CEO that he wanted to give the gift of the services of Calvin Edwards & Company if the organization was willing to be subject to due diligence. "They decided that we would perform due diligence on the organization and also prepare a business plan for an initiative that was just a dream in the mind of the CEO founder," Calvin says. "We flew out to their offices and met in a board room to go over the new plans, but there was nothing on the table. 'What do you want to do?'

I asked the CEO, and he pulled out a crumpled piece of yellow note paper from his pocket. He'd drawn three circles and written a word in each and a few bullet points underneath. He laid that on the table, talked for 30 minutes, and said 'That's what I want to do.' That's all we had to start with."

From there they worked together—Calvin, his donor client, his colleagues, and the CEO founder—to create a prospectus funded by the donor client. They ended up with a 35-page document that the donor then took to his country club buddies. He came back 60 days later with $1.35 million to fund the founder's dream. "He couldn't have raised that with the piece of yellow paper that started the process. That gift was transformative for the organization," Calvin says. "That's a donor being smart and leveraging his resources to the tune of over a million dollars."

These are just a few examples of how it's possible to multiply the value of your material resources. When you connect with an organization's leaders and fully understand their goals, chances are that your heart and head will be engaged. When this happens, leverage and overlapping ideas begin to flow, often leading to the conclusion that there are others who care as you do.

> When you connect with an organization's leaders and fully understand their goals, chances are that your heart and head will be engaged.

## Multiplying Impact by Giving Upstream

There's a familiar folk story about a group of villagers saving babies who are floating down the river and building clinics and orphanages for them, until one day a leader says, "Why don't we go upstream and stop the people who are putting these babies in the river?"

*Giving upstream* is a way of multiplying the value of your currencies by increasing the reach of your gifts. The idea is that you identify a problem that you want to tackle and then look for the root causes of the problem as far upstream as you can go. You spend your currencies on addressing those root causes rather than just treating the symptoms downstream.

Remember the starfish story? Did you have some impatience with settling for saving a few starfish here or there, even if it makes a difference to those few? Then you will love giving upstream by finding out why those starfish are suffering and rescuing all of them in one go or making sure they're never stranded again.

Doing what they call *upriver prevention* is very important to Harville Hendrix and Helen LaKelly Hunt. Harville says, "I live in the grandiose delusion that I'm actually changing the world and that the world will be better as a result of what we've done. When couples improve their relational satisfaction, that impacts on many of the various forms of suffering in the world that are caused by stressed relationships. Most other systems clean up the mess caused by stressed couples. If we can ever reach a tipping point, where healthy couples produce healthy children who run our institutions in the future, institutions would then be humane rather than inhumane. War and prisons and corporations and churches, all those institutions would be influenced by healthy people." Helen also includes in this her work in making marriage safe for women, so they can achieve their fullness inside marriage as well as outside. I love Harville and Helen's vision of transforming society into an empathetic, caring civilization.

Frank Hanna came to the upstream strategy in college. He was always interested in politics as a teenager and got involved in campaigns in college, where he noticed that most people had already determined where they were politically by the time they reached their early 20s. "There aren't a lot of adults changing their minds," Frank says, "which means that the worldview and thoughts that affect how we vote are formed earlier. Once I realized that, I thought, 'It has to start before.' If you believe that our society could be healthier and that changes must happen for that to occur, then you are more likely to effect changes if you work on culture than on the ballot box." Frank decided that the place for him to work on culture was in education and character formation for kids in kindergarten to twelfth grade.

I will stake a claim that downstream work, which focuses on relieving pain and solving problems, is less effective in the long run than upstream work, which looks to eliminate the causes of those problems. There's a need for both, but those who want to take their generosity to the next level will be looking to create lasting widespread change by giving upstream.

> Those who want to take their generosity to the next level will be looking to create lasting widespread change by giving upstream.

# Study in Generosity: Gordon Hartman

I was very interested to meet Gordon Hartman through my sister, Anne, who works for his family foundation. Gordon is a skilled developer and spent the first half of his life building successful businesses: from the landscaping operation he started in his teens to the land development company he founded at 23 that has since become the largest locally-owned homebuilding and land development enterprise in San Antonio.

Now Gordon has found a unique way to mesh his business acumen with his desire to create inclusive spaces for people with special needs. The results are extraordinary—a real testament to the power of spending one's renewable currencies on generosity that grows from a heart's desire.

Growing up in the Hartman household, Gordon witnessed countless instances of selfless generosity. His mom regularly put in extra hours at her job as a school secretary, and his father, a public servant, worked 60- and 70-hour weeks, often unpaid. Even on the nights when young Gordon stayed up well after his bedtime, he rarely saw his parents put down the work they did—not for money, but because of their commitment to their community.

## Finding His Heart's Desire

At 41, thanks to a combination of hard work, talent, and dash of luck, Gordon sold all five of his thriving businesses and retired very comfortably. With ample room in his schedule, he considered what he wanted to do next. "I wanted to spend the second half of my life giving back," he says. "From an early age, I was blessed with the talent of knowing how to make money. Then there came a point where I was asking, 'What's the real meaning of all this?' And what I came to was, 'Where much has been given, much is required.'"

One boon of early retirement was that Gordon got to spend more time with his young daughter. Morgan, the only child of Gordon and his wife, Maggie, was born with cognitive delays and physical disabilities. With therapists and doctors to support her, Gordon felt that Morgan was one of the lucky ones. As he developed relationships with Morgan's friends, and her friends' parents and caregivers, he saw firsthand how deep the needs ran for families and individuals coping with disability.

Inspired by their love for their daughter, Gordon and Maggie founded the Gordon Hartman Family Foundation. They put an initial $10 million in seed money into the Foundation to support its mission of providing support to local organizations serving those with physical and cognitive special needs.

A missed opportunity for friendship brought Gordon's mission as a philanthropist into sharp focus. While on vacation in 2006, Gordon watched 12-year-old Morgan struggling to engage with a group of kids as they goofed around in the hotel pool. He resisted intervening when he saw the group, unsure of how to interact with his daughter, walk away. The look of hurt rejection on Morgan's face was hard for him to accept. Right then and there he knew he had to figure out a way for all kids of all abilities to learn to play together.

## Gathering His Currencies

Gordon envisioned an ultra-inclusive theme park replete with rides and attractions designed to be seamlessly accessed by those with physical and cognitive challenges as well as their friends and family. The goal was simple; by creating a space where everyone could connect through play, Gordon hoped to break through barriers of misunderstanding about people with special needs and create connections that would carry over into everyday life. The park would be fun, but it would also promote awareness of the special needs community, and that awareness, in turn, would lead to more instances of inclusion in the wider world.

What Gordon wanted to build had simply never been built before, but once his vision was in place, he was determined to see it come alive. Every aspect of the park needed to be custom-designed. He started from scratch. Luckily, Gordon had the right connections with local architects and building professionals, as well as with families, medical professionals, and educators of those with special needs. With these communities at the table—some 400 people in all—Morgan's Wonderland began to take shape.

A carousel sunk into the ground to be wheelchair accessible, flashing lights to signal the start of a ride for the hearing impaired, a Sensory Village without the bright lights and loud noises that can overwhelm those with autism—all ideas were considered and fine-tuned. Plans for the park were redrawn 60 times, until all the kinks were worked out.

One detail that Gordon was adamant about from the start: the park would be free for those with special needs and inexpensive for their loved ones. Fully aware of how expensive proper care was for those with special needs, Gordon saw many families forsake fun to be able to pay for the necessary surgeries and support. He wanted Morgan's Wonderland to be a place for play, free of worry about costs.

However, Morgan's Wonderland was projected to cost upwards of $35 million, so some serious fundraising was in order. Since there was nothing like it in the world, one of the initial challenges was to convey to people the value of a theme park where barriers between those with and without special needs fall away.

## Harnessing the Multiplier Effect

> One woman wanted to help so much that she wrote a check for $20 and asked if they wouldn't mind delaying the deposit for one month; she wanted to make sure there was enough in her account.

Once people understood the concept, donations began first to trickle and then to pour in. Some were large sums, and others were whatever folks could manage. One woman wanted to help so much that she wrote a check for $20 and asked if they wouldn't mind delaying the deposit for one month; she wanted to make sure there was enough in her account. A little girl in California sold her rock collection and sent $5.31 in the mail.

Gordon found that the same multiplier effect that took over the fundraising process also took over the planning process. More and more people began giving their time to make the park a reality. In April 2010, just 39 months after its conception, Morgan's Wonderland opened with 25 custom-built rides and attractions on 25 acres.

Although the donations were generous and helpful, they weren't going to be enough to sustain the inexpensive cost of entry, but Gordon had planned for that. When he bought more than 100 acres of abandoned limestone quarry in northeast San Antonio, his plans were much larger than Morgan's Wonderland. In fact, the park's main revenue stream would come from the 75 acres adjacent to it, which Gordon slowly turned into 13 plush soccer fields called the South Texas Area Regional (STAR) Soccer Complex.

Although both the park and the complex fall under the umbrella of SOAR Inc.—the nonprofit Gordon founded—they are run with business savvy. For Gordon, the desire was to serve as many people as he could, and the best way he knew to do this was by using his finely honed strengths as a businessman. As a result, Gordon's model is simple, unique, and effective: the STAR complex generates revenue that supports Morgan's Wonderland, allowing it to be a vessel for Gordon's desire to give to the special needs community. Together, Gordon calls his operations Soccer for a Cause.

Never one to see limits, Gordon's passion continues to fuel projects that serve. In 2011, Monarch Academy opened its doors. On the grounds of Morgan's Wonderland, the Academy is a school for youth and young adults with special needs. Grounded in the belief that, with the proper support, those with special needs can actively contribute their gifts and talents to their communities, Monarch provides job and vocational training alongside an ABC education. Twenty-five young people enrolled in Monarch's first year; Gordon's dream is to serve hundreds of students every year.

If you were to ask Gordon Hartman to compare his business projects to his equally ambitious philanthropic work, he would tell you that both require long days, and he used to come home from work exhausted, physically and mentally drained. "I'm working just as much now on projects just as big," he says, but the difference is that "when I leave there's a skip in my walk and a desire to come back the next day." He feels spiritually fulfilled in a way that is beyond the power of another dollar and he has come to know the feeling of completely dedicating one's life to generosity.

> "When I leave there's a skip in my walk and a desire to come back the next day."

# Part III: The Generosity Gameplan

Jim really wants to work with the urban poor, especially those with an interest in building a small business to serve their community. That was the story of his family for three generations.

Lauren has a heart for the disenfranchised elderly. She was raised by her grandmother, who was eventually forgotten by other extended family members. And her daughter's experiences in the arts and relief for the marginalized will also influence her Generosity Gameplan.

Jim and Lauren wonder how they can turn these passions into charitable giving and volunteering opportunities. They want a clear strategy that will guide their decisions and focus their efforts.

In early discussions between Jim and Lauren about where they will focus their generous energy, they discover places of divergence and overlap. Jim is well connected in the city and can gain access to the most capable people who have a promising business idea and opportunity yet need coaching and investment. In almost every case, these individuals have elderly parents who are in need of help. So this is where they start, and the spiral of good is accelerating.

Lauren is clearly set on serving the elderly, but what is she to do with missionary work and the arts in the back of her mind? It dawns on her that the arts and missions really belonged to her daughters' hearts, so Jim and Lauren make plans in their estate to allow the daughters to be charitable in these areas while they focus on matters of their own hearts.

In Part III, we'll walk through a seven-step process that will help Jim and Lauren—and you—create a gameplan for a generous life.

# Chapter 11

# Step 1: Explore Your Heart and History

If these last chapters stirred you up about the prospect of transformational generosity, I want to channel that excitement into action by leading you through the seven-step process I developed called the Generosity Gameplan. This process forms the core of my work with clients who are taking their generosity to the next level.

**The Generosity Gameplan is all about connecting with people, projects, and causes that engage your heart.**

This process will help you map out a personalized strategy to guide your decisions and allocate your currencies in the most desirable places.

With a Generosity Gameplan, your giving takes on new characteristics:

- Your giving is **intentional** rather than reactionary, which makes your gifts more powerful and focused.

- Your giving is **individual** rather than generic. Your gifts are an expression of your true self, the person God made you to be.

- Your giving is **meaningful** rather than haphazard. You have a sense that your gifts are part of a larger purpose and they give you great satisfaction.

Before you picked up this book, you may never have considered creating a giving strategy. Perhaps you just wrote checks, showed up at meetings, and never thought about the possibility of being generous in a different way. Many people aren't aware that there are professionals who can help them get clarity about their charitable giving and volunteering. Kent Bergemann says, "Generosity isn't a topic we talk about with our friends. We never sit down with a couple over dinner and share our thoughts about giving." His wife, Linda, agrees: "For the first time in our married lives, we have a chance to volunteer together. But how do we as a couple want to share our time? How do you make decisions? How do you prioritize?"

It's simple, really: the Generosity Gameplan process will help you have those conversations and answer these seven questions— for yourself and with your spouse, your children, your friends, or whoever you'd like to engage on the subject:

- Where has my generous heart been?

- What might be holding me back from connected generosity?

- With whom and with what can I be generous?

- What makes my heart stir?

- How will I have a generous heart?

- What will I do first?

- How do the results align with my heart's desire?

The exercises included here suggest what to do, but not how. You could journal in solitude, take a weekend retreat with your spouse to explore and discuss together, or form a small group that works on one step of the Generosity Gameplan each week. Take the approach that works best for your strengths and personality.

So let's begin.

Step 1 is to **explore your heart and history.** The goal of this step is to know yourself and your heart well so you can connect and give from your heart's desire. In this step, you'll answer this question: **Where has my generous heart been?**

To arrive at the answer to this first question, we'll inquire: What life experiences have shaped you? What values do you strive to embody, and how do they affect your decisions? What are your personal and professional goals? How does your history affect your outlook on the world? Is there a greater purpose for your time on earth?

Many of us who were raised in families where faith was central to generosity may find it unusual to look at ourselves first. Isn't giving supposed to be sacrificial? Shouldn't we focus on others' needs rather than our own desires?

Responding to others' needs is the essence of charity, but when your giving is disconnected from your own heart, you can be left isolated. Exploring your heart and history is not self-centered or a waste of time, but an ideal way to amplify your innate desire to share and help others. Your heart's desire is your uniqueness and a centerpiece for action. Indeed, this is where God rests.

**The best of ourselves is decoded by discovering and claiming our heart and history.**

> Your heart's desire is your uniqueness and a centerpiece for action. Indeed, this is where God rests.

## Exercise 1: Telling Your Story

One way to explore your heart and history is to tell the story of your life to someone you trust. I want you to do this early in the process because it forms the foundation of your giving.

Here are some areas for you to explore:

- Childhood and upbringing

- Schooling

- Career path

- How you see money and resources

- The importance of relationships

- Hobbies and recreational interests

- Family life

- Community involvement

- Travel

- Spirituality

You may wonder what some of these areas have to do with generosity, but that's where the fun comes in. You never know what detail from your story will spark an interesting connection. And you'll jog your memory about important experiences you may not have thought of in years.

When you tell your story to a trusted person who can be present and listen actively, that is an amazing experience. Tell the story of your life either by writing it out ahead of time and reading it, or by narrating it directly to your chosen companion. You could progress by decades or use the theme areas listed here.

Include positive events as well as difficult times. Notice how the challenges you've faced have helped you develop some of your greatest strengths.

## Exercise 2: Your History of Generosity

Get more specific by digging into your history of generosity—from your formal philanthropy and volunteering to your amazingly ordinary generosity, the informal acts of kindness you practice daily.

Dr. Schervish calls this your *moral biography of wealth:* all the ways in which your capacities, not just your money, have combined with your conscience to shape how you serve the world. He says that people of means and substance "have the capacity, and the power, to shape the lives of others. They are potential 'hyperagents' . . . founders of the institutional framework within which they and others live and work. Their wealth makes them world-builders. And with that comes tremendous responsibility, because that capacity has the potential to have a very positive impact, or a very harmful one. The greater the capacity, the more attention that needs to be placed on how to use those resources wisely."[19] What a stirring call to follow a strategic process like the Generosity Gameplan!

> People of means and substance "have the capacity, and the power, to shape the lives of others. They are potential 'hyperagents'."

For your own history of generosity, identify key elements that have influenced your giving in past, present, and future.

- **People:** Who has been a positive role model or teacher in generosity for you? Who has given you examples you don't want to follow? Who do you want to pass your generous values on to?

- **Ideas:** What principles or beliefs have you adopted that guide your decisions about giving? What writers or speakers have influenced your thinking about generosity?

- **Charities:** What organizations have you donated to and/ or volunteered with? What are your reasons for giving to each organization?

- **Emotions:** When have you given out of joy, fear, anger, or boredom? How did your giving make you feel afterward?

- **Events:** What life experiences have prompted insights and growth in your history of generosity? Which have left you stalled? What events do you want to ensure or avoid in the future?

## Explore Your Heart and History: An Example

My friend Dave Romoser shared a good part of his history of generosity with me, and I offer some of what he said here as an example of what this first step looks like.

- Dave's father was a minister who always emphasized that what we have is "on loan from the Lord."

- Dave spent his career in legal services, the last 25 years as general counsel for two publicly held corporations.

- He has been married to Gael for 48 years and has three adult daughters, the oldest of whom is adopted.

- "On volunteering, I don't say no very well. I'm very susceptible to causes that I think are important," Dave says. "I've always had a heart for volunteering, from high school and college through to today."

- Dave has donated to organizations that were instrumental in his personal development. His undergraduate university and law school and organizations like the YMCA were a big part of his life. As he rose to a senior level as an executive, he felt more pressure to give to charities that his company and bosses were supporting. In his second half of life, he's become more focused, and most of his giving is to faith-based organizations that are delivering community and human services.

- Dave believes that he has a role as a trustee of his adopted daughter's life, so he and Gael have a strong interest in adoption and have supported the adoption agency they used.

- Dave always felt a tension between being generous with his money and talents outside the home versus meeting his family time commitments and needs for financial security. "Gael has been very good at reminding me when I was stepping over the line," he says.

- Dave's interest in supporting educational institutions is waning. He's become disappointed with law schools, which he feels are looking out for their own self-interest and doing harm to impressionable students. He has stopped giving to the university after 40 years because he and Gael feel that it has lost its vision.

- Dave and Gael experience resentment because they get so many solicitations from organizations they have supported in the past. Dave is worried about the societal impact of this saturation of mailings and cold calls. "Here we are, favorably inclined toward giving, and we're starting to resent it. What's the wider reaction going to be? People may stop giving," he says.

• Dave doesn't like to get recognition for his donations and volunteering—he finds it annoying and uncomfortable. He received an award from his Rotary chapter (an award that he thought should have acknowledged Gael's contribution as well), but he didn't want to go to the annual meeting banquet to accept it. Gael talked him into it, saying, "You're setting an example for other people."

All of these observations and anecdotes are useful in the creation of a Generosity Gameplan. In this first step, you don't need to do anything but collect and consider this information—the patterns and new directions will unfold as we go along.

## Chapter 12

# Step 2: Claim Your Generosity Gaps

In exploring your heart and history, you may have noticed times when your generosity was being held back. These insights are valuable, because only when you claim your own Generosity Gaps can you begin to close them.

- Are you telling yourself it's not the right time to get serious about giving? That's the **Action Gap.** This gap has you waiting and watching.

- Are you concerned that you won't have enough time or resources if you take your giving to the next level? That's the **Accumulation Gap.** In this gap, you're worrying.

- Are you questioning the significance of your giving efforts? Feeling worn-out and disillusioned? That's the **Gratification Gap.** This gap finds you wondering and questioning.

Step 2 is to **claim your Generosity Gaps.** The goal is to notice the distance between your generous intentions and actions and understand why the gap is there. The question is this: **What might be holding me back from connected generosity?**

I encourage you to undertake this step without self-judgment. Instead, acknowledge the difference you've made, the good you've done, *and* your desire to do

> Acknowledge the difference you've made, the good you've done, *and* your desire to do and be more.

and be more. Give thanks for having arrived at a moment when you can deepen your commitment to generosity. Stay open and curious to what your experience of the Generosity Gaps can tell you about how to move forward.

## Exercise 3: Name Your Generosity Gaps

You may already know which Generosity Gaps stall your progress, but for the sake of learning more, I'd like you to get specific and describe how the Generosity Gaps are showing up for you in relation to your longing to be more generous.

*1. Your desire to give*

List the ways in which you would like to take your giving to the next level. Using all of your currencies, think about your opportunities to be generous. Here are some example goals you might want to pursue:

- I'd like to build closer, deeper relationships with a few important people.

- I'd like to measure the results of my giving rather than measuring what I give.

- I'd like to consider making contributions that build personal or organizational bandwidth.

- I'd like to encourage and empower people to exchange ideas, solutions, and connections.

- I'd like to overlap my efforts with other people who care as I do.

## 2. The gaps between longing and action

For each longing you listed, identify why you haven't acted on that longing yet. Be as detailed as possible. Then see if you can name the Generosity Gap that each reason represents. Go back to Chapters 4, 5, and 6 to remind yourself about the three Generosity Gaps if you need to. Here are some examples:

- Work has been demanding, and I'm tired when I get home. (Action Gap)

- I'm worried that my spouse thinks that we're already too generous, and I don't want to have that conversation. (Accumulation Gap)

- I don't know how to prioritize when everything seems urgent and necessary. (Gratification Gap)

- I'm concerned that I'll be asked for more than I can handle. (Action Gap)

- I'm unsure about building bridges for my friends—who do they need to know that I know? (Gratification Gap)

- I don't know how much to provide for my children and what I will have left over. (Accumulation Gap)

## 3. A snapshot of what you think and feel

Describe what it's like to be in these Generosity Gaps—the thoughts and feelings you have. This is your Before snapshot—a baseline that you can compare yourself to after you finish the Generosity Gameplan process. Your Before snapshot may look something like this:

- When I think about doing generosity together with my spouse, the first thing that comes to mind is our differences. I feel disappointed that we're not on the same page when it comes to giving.

- When I see the third annual appeal from one of my favorite charities, I feel frustrated. I wonder, *do they realize I have already made a contribution?*

- When I say yes to another committee assignment, I have second thoughts after the first meeting. I don't feel like I can play a vital role.

- When I see a good friend after a long absence, I remember I promised to introduce him to another and have yet to fulfill the pledge, and I feel embarrassed.

Now, congratulate yourself and take the rest of the day off! It's not easy to take an unflinching look at your Generosity Gaps, but you'll thank yourself for it later.

## Exercise 4: Step out of the Generosity Gaps

**Awareness is the prelude to change.**

The good news is that just naming and describing your Generosity Gaps goes a long way to addressing them. Awareness is the prelude to change. This next exercise will point you towards your path out of the Generosity Gaps.

### 1. Take on a posture of gratitude

Remembering and appreciating what you have received is important preparation for generosity. Who has packed your parachute? What graces have you been given? There are lots of creative ways to count your blessings:

- Pick a time each day to be aware, appreciative, and attentive.

- Look through family photos.

- Take a walk through your home and neighborhood.

- Make a list of all the people who have touched your life.

## 2. Own your Generosity Gaps

Acknowledge that you are stalled in the Generosity Gaps you've identified. You can't start from anywhere except where you are, so there's power in acknowledging that starting point. Remember that you are building on your progress and no longer comparing yourself to perfection.

## 3. Choose to act

You know that the purpose of doing something small is to get moving. Remind yourself how easy it is and how good it feels to give by doing one small thing to close the Generosity Gap. Here are a few things you could try:

- Build a relationship bridge by introducing two people who would benefit from knowing each other (see the exercise on Relationships as Currency in Chapter 13 for more details on how to do this.)

- Spend what you're good at by helping the next person you come across who needs advice or service.

- Give away a small resource that you've been holding tightly.

There! That one small act will be the first of many, and you'll be amazed where it will take you.

## Claim Your Generosity Gaps: An Example

For many years, Helen LaKelly Hunt did fundraising for women's organizations. She would ask a woman to give a five-figure gift to the women's organization in her city, and the woman would say, "Let me think about it," or "Let me ask my husband." Then she'd come back and say, "I can make that contribution," and Helen would say, "Thank you, thank you." These were welcome gifts, but they had something of a transactional quality—cool and quiet.

Then, Helen co-created Women Moving Millions, and she and other Women Moving Millions donors began asking women to make million-dollar pledges. "I can't tell you the number of women who teared up when they said they would do it, and they thanked me!" Helen says. "I'd ask them for $100,000 a year for 10 years and they'd start crying and say, 'Thank you, thank you, thank you!'"

I can only speculate, but I imagine that some of these women were in the Action Gap, waiting for a time in the future when they could get organized to make a major gift like Helen asked for. Some were probably in the Accumulation Gap, worrying that they didn't have access to enough until Women Moving Millions inspired them to question that assumption. And some were likely in the Gratification Gap, routinely making smaller donations but wondering whether those donations really mattered.

Helen wanted to know why she had women thanking her when she asked them for a million dollars, so she asked a psychologist about it. "She said that I had invited these women into their power. They'd been disassociated from their own power, and in stepping into their power, they became whole, because they *could* be that generous. They *could* share that way but they weren't, because it was too big a number. And suddenly they realized, *I can do this!*"

I can just sense the satisfaction of the transformational generosity at work here—both in Helen's bold challenge and in these women's passionate response. The same powerful transformation is waiting for you as you claim and close your Generosity Gaps.

# Chapter 13

# Step 3: Count Your Currencies

Most of us would say that a good way to manage money is to know our assets, income, and expenses so that we can budget to cover costs and judiciously spend and invest the surplus. Yet many people do the opposite when it comes to charitable giving and volunteering. They wait until they're asked to give time and money, do a cursory check to see if they have enough in their schedule or account to cover the cost, and make a one-off decision to say yes or no.

How much more empowering would it be to add up all your renewable currencies and allocate them with thoughtful purpose? In other words, the question becomes this: **With whom and with what can I be generous?**

Step 3 is to **count your currencies.** The goal is to know what you have to give so you can direct your gifts toward the things you care about most.

- What **relationships** form your network of business, social, and family ties?

- What **strengths** are inherent in your personality, and what skills have you developed through practice that can help others?

- What **resources** of money, time, space, and possessions can you leverage to do good?

## Exercise 5: Remember Your Relationships

Chances are that you have developed more relationships and friendships over time than you can possibly cultivate. Here's a way to identify the key people in your life.

### 1. Who am I in the world?

Reflect on who you are in the world. What roles do you play, and what are you called? For example, I made a list of 62 words that describe me, starting with father, husband, Texan, and Wisconsinite, and ending with fly fisherman, camper, and dog owner.

### 2. The nearest three people

With each role, who are two or three people who come to your mind right away? Taken altogether, these people form your core network.

(Is your number around 150 people? This wouldn't be surprising, since psychologist Robin Dunbar has studied social networks and determined that "most [people] cannot maintain many more than 150 meaningful relationships. Cognitively, we're just not built for it.")[20]

You could stop at this point in the exercise, but why not take it further and try building some relationship bridges? Among the people you've identified, many have at least one thing in common. Perhaps they have similar life experiences, challenges, and solutions that overlap, a set of talents, or connections that could be the last tumbler that falls into place to unlock an opportunity.

### 3. Name your top ten

Look over the list of people. Trust your intuition. For those you know well, who might they need to meet for their mutual benefit, not yours? You will discover that there are some people you're out of touch with and do not know well anymore but would like to.

Here's your chance to prioritize and get started, acquaint yourself with them, or get reconnected. Be present.

### 5. Build the bridge

Choose your introduction method. In person? By telephone? Often email works beautifully. Tell each person about the other and why you thought of putting them in touch.

### 6. Circle back and repeat

In time, follow up and see if the connection happened. Your intent is to be generous, not intrusive, but it is possible that the people you are connecting will need encouragement from you.

Now celebrate, and make bridge-building a habit!

## Exercise 6: Assess Your Strengths

I'm willing to bet that you know very well what you're good at. You don't usually get to a place of success in career and relationships unless you have some awareness of your natural talents and traits.

If you want more insight and clarity, I highly recommend diagnostics like the Clifton StrengthsFinder and the Myers-Briggs personality assessment. Take a few minutes to recall and write down what you know about your strengths—at work, at home, and in social situations.

Spiritual gifts are a type of strength that people often haven't thought much about. Spiritual gifts are freely given. When we live out of these gifts, we are more like our true selves, and when we give them away, we fulfill an often unacknowledged longing. There are several ways to assess what you are called to and gifted for. I particularly like the method developed by the Catherine of Sienna Institute. Focusing just on the gifts that are service-oriented, consider which of these roles you are particularly inspired by and drawn to.

- **Administration:** Planning and coordinating to accomplish good things

- **Craftsmanship:** Artistic and creative work that orders our world

- **Encouragement:** Nurturing others through your presence

- **Healing:** Channeling God's gift of restoration

- **Hospitality:** Warmth and welcoming, food, shelter, clothing

- **Knowledge:** Studying to understand ourselves and others

- **Service:** Recognizing unmet needs that prevent good things from happening

- **Teaching:** Enabling others to learn and reach their potential

- **Wisdom:** Remarkable insight that enables good decisions

- **Mercy:** Comforting others with empathy

> Be honest with yourself about what you're good at. Then you can really use your strengths instead of just giving away your time.

The most important takeaway when considering spiritual gifts and other strengths is to be honest with yourself about what you're good at. Then you can really use your strengths instead of just giving away your time. Later in the

Generosity Gameplan process, you'll analyze where you're giving service and decide whether that service is drawing out the best in you.

## Exercise 7: Inventory Your Resources

I believe that being generous with resources has less to do with how much you give and more to do with where the money goes and how it's working. So when you consider what portion of your balance sheet is available, consider the results you can achieve as much or more than the amount you give.

I also want you to go beyond money to consider the other resources you have:

- **Possessions:** What do you own that you no longer need but that others could benefit from? Many people are finding freedom and joy in de-cluttering their lives these days.

- **Space:** Do you have room in your house or business that isn't being used? I have a friend who loans his vacation home to couples in crisis, for example.

- **Talent:** Could your business do pro bono work for a passionate social sector leader with a winning idea?

- **Assets:** What value rests in your assets that you could leverage? Perhaps cash flow is limited right now, but could you repurpose some real estate? Remember, too, that you have access to and influence over the resources of others.

When you begin your giving strategy with relationships and strengths, your decisions about where to put your resources will naturally fall into place, and you'll discover that the amount you give will be enough to achieve your generous goals.

## Count Your Currencies: An Example

Being on the receiving end of a relationship capital gift is amazing. My friend Deborah Fugenschuh, president of the Donors Forum of Wisconsin, once suggested that I meet another donor in our community. The Vine and Branches Foundation that I serve had made a gift to an inner city organization whose leadership was in crisis, and the capital we invested was at risk. Deborah knew the situation and wanted to connect me with another donor who had also made a gift to the same organization—the president of Wells Fargo Bank in Wisconsin, Kent Bergemann. I called Kent, and we met for lunch and discussed how together we might be a force for good to resolve the problems at the organization.

As we started to discuss our personal lives, we discovered remarkable similarities. We are both Catholics grounded in Ignatian spirituality, married for over 25 years with two adult children, outdoorsmen who hunt in the same county during the same week, year after year, adventure travelers, and so on. Since that day, Kent and I have been intentional and close friends, and we often invest our philanthropy together in order to leverage our collective impact. Our wives have gotten to know each other well, and together we enjoy the rare magic of genuine couple friends.

This gift that Deborah gave to me, without expecting repayment and with no knowledge of the possible personal connections, has become powerful in my life. A gift freely given generates gratitude—my gratitude to Deborah is expressed in a generous posture of building relationship bridges wherever I can.

My friends Scott and Theresa are clear on their currencies and have intentionally increased their generous ways over time. Early on, they devoted a small percentage of their energy to helping champions of healthy relationships. Now they invest the majority of their energy serving champions by building technology platforms so that people can improve relationships and collaborate. Learning from his successful and not-so-successful ventures, Scott tries to "identify that which wants to happen and help it along" rather than making something happen. For instance, he believes that, "In getting things done and creating change, collaboration should be the turbo-charge on the way out, rather than the toll on the way in."

> "Identify that which wants to happen and help it along" rather than making something happen.

Tim Watkins knows his currencies too. His company, Renegade Communications, is a strategic and creative advertising services company. When Father Leo Patalinghug came to him with an idea for a ministry called Grace Before Meals, Tim embraced the idea and gave generous in-house talent to plan and implement a robust digital strategy, website, and ongoing support to grow the ministry. All of this was accomplished using Tim's unique strengths in strategic and creative advertising services.

I hope this step in the Generosity Gameplan process gets you excited about your abundant currencies and all the creative ways you can put them into action for good.

# Chapter 14

# Step 4: React to the Headlines

In the last step, you looked at *what* you have to spend. Now we're narrowing in on where you want to spend it. This step is fundamental to connected generosity, where you give and serve others with intentionality rather than responding to the most urgent or most effectively delivered case for support.

Step 4 is to **react to the headlines.** The goal is to identify the causes and issues that you are most passionate about and answer this question: **What makes my heart stir?**

A great way to do this is to sit down with the news. When I'm listening to my heart, I find it helpful to seek out alternative news sources, different from the ones I always use. Look for what Paul Harvey used to call the *rest of the story*. Dig a little. What news makes you a bit uncomfortable? What events cause your heart rate to increase? How do you want to see the world change? In these stories, you'll find clues to the problems that might benefit from your generous impulses.

More often than not, the needs that speak most deeply to you are those that have touched your own life. This whisper might be God calling you to spend your currencies in these tender areas. Connecting generosity with your own experiences gives you empathy and energy that multiplies your efforts.

> Connecting generosity with your own experiences gives you empathy and energy that multiplies your efforts.

## Exercise 8: Consult Trusted News Sources

If you're still wondering what your heart's desire is when it comes to changing the world, this step in the process will make it abundantly clear. Current affairs, those close to home and far away, can stir up our passions like nothing else, and in this digital age, there's no shortage of opinion and information coming at us.

### 1. Collect your headlines

Spend two weeks gathering articles, stories, and news from a variety of sources. Look for the headlines that move you—news that makes you want to celebrate, get angry, or take action. Try to collect 50+ items that you would rate at an interest level of eight out of ten or higher.

Also look back at the life story and history of generosity you created in Step 1: Explore Your Heart and History. Have you missed any important issues? Search out items that reflect those as well.

### 2. Organize your headlines

Sort your items into various categories. The items you collect will create a pattern that reveals your areas of interest.

**Examples of causes**

| | |
|---|---|
| Religion/faith | Domestic or international policy |
| Poverty | Environment |
| Education | Natural disaster preparation/response |
| Health | Civil society/cultural issues |
| Human rights | Economic development |
| Child development or youth issues | Rural concerns |

Family issues

Women's and girls' issues

Men's and boys' issues

Older adult (65+) issues

Visual or performing arts

Amateur sports

Relational wellness

Scientific or medical research

Animal health/prevention of cruelty

Community service/volunteerism

Crime, violence in families or schools

Homeland security/terrorism

International security

## Examples of target groups

Infants and preschool children
(birth–age 3)

Children (ages 3–13)

High school students (ages 13–18)

College students/young adults
(ages 19–23)

Parents

Women (ages 24–64)

Men (ages 24–64)

Seniors (ages 65+)

The homeless

Workers or the unemployed

Minorities

Clergy

Teachers

Military/police/fire/EMT personnel

Amateur athletes

Musicians and other

Visual and literary artists

Immigrants

Physically challenged

Cognitively challenged

Mentally ill

Medical patients (cancer, AIDS, etc.)

Chemical and substance

Facilities/buildings

People in other countries

Wildlife/domestic pets

Waterways/oceans

Land/forests/open spaces

Earth's atmosphere

## Examples of needs

| | |
|---|---|
| Physical or emotional pain | Healthy relationships |
| Physical, emotional, sexual abuse | Single parenting |
| Public awareness of a specific issue | Financial literacy |
| Isolation/rejection | Personal empowerment to change |
| Life transition | Personal faith |
| Hunger | Overcoming illness and disease |
| Housing/shelter | Economic opportunities |
| Literacy | Habitat preservation/restoration |
| Obtaining a higher level of education | Sustaining the environment |
| Special skills or job training | Life skills/independence training |

## Examples of realms of influence

| | |
|---|---|
| International | City/County |
| National | Neighborhood |
| Regional | Other |
| Statewide | |

Solutions you seek will likely land in one or more of these worldviews:

- **Moral/religious:** If you care particularly about people's behavior and personal choices, you may seek answers in faith communities and ministries, including education.

- **Political:** If you're fascinated by the role of good public policies or interactions between nations, you may turn to campaigning, electoral reform, legislation, and inter-governmental organizations.

- **Social science:** If you know that effective solutions are grounded in quality research and discovery, you'll find solutions in testing, trying, and experimentation.

- **Business/economic:** If you're interested in how culture affects the marketplace, employee behavior, or productivity, and if you know that world events are largely driven by economic forces, you may look for solutions in the market itself.

When you've discovered your hot-button issues and your worldviews through this headline exercise, you'll know where and how you want to help.

## React to the Headlines: An Example

I introduced you to John and Sherri Kasdorf in Chapter 5 when we looked at the Accumulation Gap. You may remember that John grew up immersed in Depression-era frugality, but that he and Sherri moved beyond their fears about having enough when they explored the larger world around them with a moral religious worldview. Now I'd like to show you how they identified their own headline issues and got strategic about their generosity.

John had started a business or two after their children arrived, and the family was constantly cash poor as the businesses got up and running. "My frugal genes were kicking in," John says, "so I remember doing a deal with the Lord—we'll give 2 percent and see what happens. We just needed to put some organization and structure around it." That commitment was the first step in an intentional focus on giving.

At a Christian business meeting, John learned about Bill Eisner Sr., founder of a Milwaukee advertising agency, who contributed 10 percent of his company's profits to charity. "Eisner was formative for me," John says, "I was thinking, there's got to be a better way of integrating business with faith. I was so preoccupied with the daily demands of running a company, and I needed something that would force me to dedicate more time to charitable giving, instead of just making year-end donations." John and Sherri decided that they would create a giving entity for their business as well.

John is a do-it-yourselfer at heart; he loves to do things from scratch, and the foundation he created was no exception. He began with a few thousand dollars and took a year to deal with forms, documents, and IRS requirements to start it up.

"We decided on three criteria, because there are a million organizations that call and send you requests! And every one of them is wonderful."

Setting up the foundation required that John and Sherri identify their headline issues. I met them around this time, and I remember how thoughtful they were about their priorities. Sherri says, "We decided on three criteria, because there are a million organizations that call and send you requests! And every one of them is wonderful. I always want to give everything. But we decided that we would support groups that were 1) spreading the gospel, 2) helping people in need, and 3) operating in southeast Wisconsin. We really narrowed it down, because there are many organizations helping with food, clothing, and shelter, but we felt that if they didn't share the gospel, they didn't get to the heart of the matter."

Sherri was involved with inner city ministry through her church. Her heart was to take groups of women to work and serve directly with people downtown. They saw single mothers struggling to stay afloat in homeless shelters, children who were hungry for affection, drug users and people who had come clean. Sherri saw from the inside what John was trying to scout from the outside, so they made sure to link up so the foundation had the benefit of Sherri's experience.

Over the years their criteria have evolved, and they have expanded their concept of people in need to include children who require afterschool care and people with psychiatric needs. But their commitment to sharing the gospel is unchanged. "All of it has to offer Christ as an influence in the remediation process," John says. "We don't want to hit people over the head with the Bible, but we do want it to be part of the process.".

In the beginning, John and Sherri supported existing programs that were doing skilled work with a spiritual approach. But as the foundation matured, they also found opportunities to bring their headline issues together to create new, effective programs at secular organizations. Their foundation was solicited for several years by Rogers Memorial Hospital, a 100-year-old psychiatric facility that was very successful in a low-profile way. Initially John told the hospital that it had a wonderful purpose but that the Kasdorfs' foundation couldn't give financial support because the hospital didn't offer patients an exposure to the power of spiritual healing.

A few years later, though, Sherri and John partnered with a chaplain who had experience in clinical care for psychiatric patients. Together they devised a program that was presented with the singular goal of improving patient healing, and Rogers Memorial Hospital agreed to try it out. After two successful pilot periods of six months each, the hospital instituted a spiritual care clinical outreach as part of its remedial care.

This introduction of spiritual principles resulted in dramatically improved patient healing, and the program exploded. Sherri says, "Doctors who were against the chaplaincy program at the beginning now want their patients exposed. They can see that other patients have been so helped by it and have become much more whole. And it's spreading to other campuses of the hospital." The program is fully elective, so both the patient and the doctor must opt in to access it. "This element was critical to the program's acceptance and, ultimately, its differentiated outcome," says John.

I love how Sherri and John have been intentional and focused on what matters to them. The story of Rogers Memorial shows how they combined the **cause** of faith/spiritual healing, the **target group** of mental health patients and their families, and the **realm** of community health and safety. The Kasdorfs are confident that if they pursue what is true for them and seek out solutions that align with their worldview, change can happen. John and Sherri are no longer tipping; they are paying the tab, and they are connected for good with all their currencies.

# Chapter 15

# Step 5: Develop Your Gameplan

Perhaps at this point in the process you're feeling like developing a Generosity Gameplan is a lot of work. "I'm just trying to do something good!" you're thinking. "Why should it be so complicated?"

I hear you. Check-writing philanthropy and showing up on Volunteer Day are certainly simpler than transformational generosity. But you have your sights set higher. You want to connect heart-to-heart and be confident that your giving is effective.

"Don't expect that making decisions about giving will be easy merely because you have good intentions," says Frank Hanna. "When you buy a new car or a washer and dryer, you expect to put in the work to find the brand, model, and price you want. You research products and suppliers. So why wouldn't you make your generosity decisions with the same rigor as consumer purchases?"

Step 5 is to **develop your gameplan.** The goal is to create a strategy for spending your currencies in the areas that you care about—your headline issues—and answer the question: **How will I have a generous heart?**

You begin by considering your relationship capital. How can you help friends and family? And with whom can you be connected for good?

Next, you look to activities that allow you to use your strengths. What do you love to do, and what are you known for doing well?

Only then do you ask how you can allocate your money and other resources. All three currencies work in sync, but it's important to begin with relationships and strengths so that love, not obligation, drives your outflow of resources.

## Exercise 9: Create Your Personal Giving Mission

> When it comes to your generosity, you aren't just making a statement—you are on a mission to change your world.

Perhaps you've helped create a clear vision for a business, church, or other organization. It's likely that you created a mission statement to describe that vision. I like to drop the word *statement* from this phrase. Why? When it comes to your generosity, you aren't just making a statement—you are on a mission to change your world. Your mission is specific and serves to make your gameplan more powerful and compelling.

What you leave out of your mission is as important as what you include. Choosing can be difficult when you have wide interests or want to stay open to possibilities. But it's easier to say no here and now to causes and organizations that don't touch your heart. Remember that it's better to go narrow and deep than wide and shallow.

Take your time and practice writing your mission, and when you are clear, you can confidently tell others about it. If you'll be giving with others (your family or your spouse, for example), write independently at first and then see what common ground exists. If you find divergent interests, don't worry. Make room in your gameplan for these differences at first and practice finding common ground.

Elements you could include in your personal giving mission:

- The causes, target groups, and needs that you identified in Step 4 (your headline issues)

- The realm of influence and worldview you embrace, also from Step 4

- The type of nonprofit organizations you want to partner with:

| | |
|---|---|
| Church or synagogue | Public or private educational institution |
| Faith-based ministry group outside of church | Hospital or medical facility |
| General nonprofit organization | Government agency |
| Other | |

- The organizational orientation you favor:

| | |
|---|---|
| Prevention | Health/recovery after |
| Early intervention | Multiple approaches |
| Late intervention/rescue | |

- The organizational nature of the nonprofits you prefer to work with:

| | |
|---|---|
| Large and established | Grassroots and loosely structured |
| Small and established | Innovative and entrepreneurial |
| Established but in decline, needs assistance for turn-around | Visionary organization in start-up or growth phase |

Here is a sample mission for personal giving:

> *I feel strongly about helping causes related to education and relational wellness that specifically address the needs of high school and college students who need to learn conflict resolution, communication, and commitment. I envision fulfilling my generous goals with schools and nonprofit organizations that are committed to whole, thriving students, that are small and established in nature, and whose area of influence is focused on my city.*

## Exercise 10: Evaluate Your Current Giving

Now, how does your charitable giving and volunteering compare to the personal giving mission you just created?

Start by taking a snapshot of your current giving, and then evaluate it based on the heart-led focus you've developed.

### 1. Create a summary

What do you give now?

- How are you spending your **relationships**? Where have you built bridges? Who are you giving your presence and attention to?

- How are you spending your **strengths**? What volunteering do you do? How much time do you invest?

- How are you spending your **resources**? What charitable gifts do you make, both one-time and ongoing? What bequests have you arranged for your estate? How do you give your other material possessions and leverage your assets?

### 2. Evaluate

For each generous act, ask these questions:

- Does it contribute to one of your headline issues—a cause that is close to your heart?

- How connected are you to the people involved? Have you developed good relationships or is your involvement mostly impersonal?

- Are you spending your strengths in the volunteering you do? Do you feel energized or drained by your involvement?

- Do you know what your financial donations are being used for? Have you seen the impact of the organization's work?

### 3. Identify the gifts that don't fit

Take note of any charitable gifts and volunteering efforts that don't belong in your Generosity Gameplan for these reasons:

- They don't match your personal giving mission.

- They don't contribute to your heart's desire for connection and change.

- They don't involve spending your relationships and strengths.

## Exercise 11: Dream

I hope that some of the stories I've included in this book, and the ones you've come across in the media and your personal networks, have sparked ideas about what you could do when you take your generosity to the next level.

At this point in the process, I want you to let your imagination run free. Without censoring yourself or worrying about feasibility, brainstorm all the ways you could create the kind of change you want to see. Challenge your spouse to see who can come up with the most outrageous or innovative idea. Return to the longings of your childhood—did you have a wild plan for service that you later gave up as impractical or too difficult?

> Without censoring yourself or worrying about feasibility, brainstorm all the ways you could create the kind of change you want to see.

Consider each of the elements of your personal giving mission in turn. Is there an organization you've always admired? A need in your target group that makes you wonder, *Why isn't someone filling this need in this way?* Perhaps you've had a negative experience in your giving and you dream of doing things differently.

Capture each of these dreams in whatever way you're inspired to.

## Exercise 12: Draw Up Your Gameplan

Now it's time to pull all the pieces of your Generosity Gameplan together. When you finish this exercise, you'll have a step-by-step strategy to follow.

### 1. Where will you stop giving?

Decide which existing charitable donations and volunteering commitments you will discontinue. Create a plan for when and how you will wrap up those responsibilities.

Leaving a post or ending a contribution can be challenging to consider, but you cannot make room for transformational generosity unless you first weed out the transactional giving. Think of this process as reinvesting your currencies from a low-return investment into one that has a higher yield. You'll be devoting the same resources but life will be better for you and others.

Remember that in a diversified approach to giving, you want 80 percent of your giving to go to the 20 percent of causes and projects that are most important to you. You can keep some commitments that fall outside of your mission, such as your next-door neighbor's favorite charity or your alma mater, but make sure they are in proper proportion to your heart-centered initiatives.

> Think of this process as reinvesting your currencies from a low-return investment into one that has a higher yield.

### 2. Consider your relationship capital

Bring out the list of people you made in Step 3—Count Your Currencies and follow these steps:

- Acknowledge the people that you give to daily: your family and close friends. Reflect on how to give them your presence and help them solve their challenges and maximize their own strengths through amazingly ordinary generosity.

- Note the people that you want to build relationship bridges for.

- Identify those who are connected to your headline issues. Connect with these leaders, discuss the solutions that are on the horizon, and consider becoming engaged with them.

### 3. Plan your volunteering

Think about your phase of life and your schedule, and then answer these questions:

- How much time do you have to devote to volunteering?

- What types of volunteering activities take advantage of your strengths? Are you drawn to one-on-one mentoring, administration, promotion and outreach, or leadership?

- What organizations do you want to work with on the ground? These may be groups that you've been involved with previously or new ones that you discover through research and talking to those in your network. What kind of volunteer support do they need?

- Decide which volunteer opportunities you will pursue.

### 4. Allocate your resources

Determine where to put your funds as well as your space, possessions, and assets:

- In consultation with your spouse and your financial adviser, answer the question, "How much is enough?" The excess that remains is freedom with which to be generous. This step, of course, is oversimplified to make a point. That is, most of us have never really answered that question.

- Investigate the material needs of the organizations you are volunteering with, as well as the needs of other groups that address your headline issues.

- Match up your resources with the needs you've identified. Remember that a few larger gifts are usually preferable to many smaller gifts. (That said, I do know two people who decided to never say no. So they say yes with micro-gifts to anyone who asks.) Remember also that the more engaged you are with the people involved, and the more you spend your strengths in service, the better decisions you'll make about contributing your resources.

- Consider establishing a foundation or a donor-advised fund to distribute your contributions.

I've only covered the basics of developing your Generosity Gameplan here, so take your time and invest in thoughtful reflection, which is the key to success. Those people with the most life-giving gameplans are those who follow writer Dorothea Brande's advice, "Act boldly and unseen forces will come to your aid."

> "Act boldly and unseen forces will come to your aid."

# Chapter 16

# Step 6: Get in the Game

*"Well begun is half done."* Proverb quoted by Aristotle

Now that you have a Generosity Gameplan, how do you feel about putting your generosity into play? You might be eager to get going and certain of your next moves. Or you might feel a little overwhelmed by what lies ahead. You may want more information or support as you make changes in the way you give.

Step 6 is to **get in the game.** The goal is to execute the strategies laid out in your Generosity Gameplan. In this step, you'll answer the question: **What will I do first?**

This phase of the process focuses on turning your generous plans into reality. All the dreams and ideas in the world are of little benefit if they stay on the page.

Getting in the game looks different for everyone, but here are some actions you might take to get started.

**Connect with the top ten most valuable relationships you identified and listen for their challenges, dreams, and currencies.**

Connecting with your top ten relationships can be done in any way you like, but it should always result in face-to-face conversations where you can really be present. Here's one question that usually gets things moving:

> As you listen, be present and listen for the challenges, dreams, and currencies your friend has.

"If we meet again in a year or so, what do you hope will have happened for you to be loving life?"

As you listen, be present and listen for the challenges, dreams, and currencies your friend has. What problems is your friend wrestling with? What longings are expressed? What relationships, strengths, and resources does your friend have to give?

And your response? Avoid trying to fix anything yourself, but think of other connections you have who might share common ground with this friend. Build a relationship bridge, trust the value of the connection, and follow up to ensure the bridge was made.

The act of generosity here is to expand the other's sphere of influence, access, and capacity.

**Resign from boards that aren't using your strengths.**

Resigning from boards or committees that are not maximizing your strengths can be tricky because you want to honor the organization you have been serving. First, make it known that you now have a clear and strategic Generosity Gameplan. Focusing only on opportunities where you can do what you do best is a well-respected posture for any generous person to have. The leaders with whom you are having this conversation will likely regret your decision but freely release you from obligation.

> Focusing only on opportunities where you can do what you do best is a well-respected posture for any generous person to have.

Second, advance notice is always helpful to a board or committee, giving the members time to find your successor. If you know of someone who can use his or her strengths in that position, building a bridge between that person and the leaders is a generous act.

**Volunteer using your strengths for a role that you discovered yourself based on one of your headline issues.**

A little extra effort will pay off if you can resist taking the first volunteer opportunity offered to you, even if happens to be in an organization you care about. Chances are that leaders in that organization are stretched to the limits and seeking what they call *capacity-building grants.* These grants help add more staff, more space, or more programs. Imagine yourself plugging into one of these pressing needs as a volunteer, serving in ways that matter to you and to them.

**Cancel your many small contributions to various organizations and send larger checks to the effective few.**

Replacing your small donations with fewer but more significant commitments makes strategic sense, but saying no is not always easy. Take your time, and when saying no, make it as personal as you can. Again, make it clear that you have a Generosity Gameplan that allows you to focus more attention on the few you are most passionate about. Great organization leaders understand this and should release you from future appeals with a blessing.

**Create a foundation or a donor-advised fund to administer major gifts in line with a larger vision you've uncovered.**

Creating a foundation or donor-advised fund does not have to be complicated, but it does require planning. These are the first four questions to answer:

- Will my generous goals take a lifetime or more to achieve?

- Over time, will my capacity to be generous increase?

- Will the problems I care about take a long time to fix, or are there one-time solutions available today?

- Will I be generous with others? Perhaps with my children?

There are exceptionally good advisors to help navigate this decision. Look for chemistry with the advisor first, and then look for expertise in the problems you want to solve. Remember that donor-advised funds and community foundations come in all shapes and sizes. Having a relationship with the fund's leaders will add to your confidence and likely to your effectiveness.

## Get in the Game: An Example

Calvin Edwards shared with me a fascinating story about David Allman, a man who has a passion for serving the poor. David is a commercial real estate developer, and for many years he gave to Christian and humanitarian causes, mostly focused in the US. But he wanted to expand his scope to giving internationally.

David knew that he wanted to work in a country that was easily accessible from his home in Atlanta so that he could build and maintain strong connections more easily. Calvin introduced him to Opportunity International, a microfinance organization, and David chose to focus his efforts in Nicaragua, which he could reach on a three-hour nonstop flight from Atlanta, only one time zone away.

> David got in the game by partnering with an existing organization that he could trust.

David worked with Opportunity International to create a unique program under their umbrella that had its own nonprofit organization—essentially a subsidiary operating solely in

Nicaragua. David sat on the board of the new organization and brought in others that he knew and trusted to serve with him. One of these supporters was a colleague from Atlanta who has an urban ministry to alleviate poverty, and he and David co-developed a pilot project. They wanted to test two poverty alleviation methodologies in combination: microfinance and community economic development. The idea was to pick a piece of geography and undertake both approaches intensively, literally on top of each other, to see whether they made a significant difference.

David went to Nicaragua three or four times a year, often with his family, who volunteered and supported the program. He also brought down new donors who came to the table. In other words, he participated in a very direct way, rather than hanging around wringing his hands, wondering what to do.

Calvin's firm was significantly involved in the concept's implementation once it was conceived. They helped write the business plan, hire the executive director, select sites, and set up evaluation systems. They put in a fair bit of work in the early days, and then the project took off on its own.

David got in the game by partnering with an existing organization that he could trust, working in a country that was accessible, creating an entity that he could direct through a board, and staying involved for five years so he could oversee the entire project from beginning to end. I'm always amazed at what unfolds when people move from idea to execution on their Generosity Gameplans.

# Chapter 17

# Step 7: Reflect on Your Results

When you're head-down and executing, it's easy to take your eyes off the bigger picture. No Generosity Gameplan will be perfect out of the gate, so it's important to slow down and evaluate. You don't have to go back to Step 1 of the process—you can build on what you've learned and reset your strategy to take you even further.

Step 7 is to **reflect on your results.** The goal is to look back on what you've done so you can celebrate and make changes where needed. In this step, you'll answer the question: **How do my results align with my heart's desire?**

The real-world impact of your giving is an important thing to look at, although it's tricky to measure. But just as important is the personal transformation. Are your relationships richer? Are your acts of service more gratifying? These are signs that you are practicing connected generosity and that the vision you outlined in your personal giving mission is truly your heart's desire.

> Just as important is the personal transformation. Are your relationships richer? Are your acts of service more gratifying?

## Exercise 14: Revisit Your Generosity Gaps

Remember that Before snapshot you took in Step 2—Claim Your Generosity Gaps? You described what it was like to be in the

Generosity Gaps—what you thought and felt. Now is the time to take your After snapshot.

What is it like to be practicing transformational generosity as laid out in your Generosity Gameplan? Your After snapshot could look like this:

- At the end of a board meeting, I am motivated and eager to get going on the decisions we made.

- When my spouse and I work together on our plans for giving, I feel a sense of gratitude and closeness.

- When I get donation requests in the mail from causes I'm not focused on, I'm relieved because I can say no purposefully.

- When someone asks me to serve on a committee, I feel free to ask questions and make sure I'm the right person for the task.

- When I consider my estate plans, I feel at peace and certain about where my bequests are going.

Your thoughts and feelings may not all be positive, and that's okay. Just notice where the Generosity Gaps are still present and keep taking action to move beyond them. What's important is progress.

Feelings of connection and gratification are particularly good signs. Celebrate! Look at where they are strongest and consider how you might amplify those areas. Perhaps you will focus even more intently on a particular organization, or free up more time and resources to devote to a certain cause.

# Exercise 15:
# Reflect on Relationships and Meaning

*1. How have your connections changed?*

Starting your generosity with relationship creates a stronger and more authentic network of friends and partners. Ask yourself these questions:

- What new relationships have developed since you started taking action on your Generosity Gameplan?

- What existing relationships have become closer and more valuable?

- What problematic relationships have fallen away?

- What are your favorite people memories—events, conversations, moments—that have occurred in the context of generosity?

- Do you feel vital and appreciated at the organizations where you give and serve?

*2. How has your sense of purpose changed?*

Listening to and working toward your heart's desire for positive change creates more meaningful acts of service. Ask yourself these questions:

- What are you proud of having accomplished or supported?

- What have you learned that will help you in the future?

- What uninspiring ventures and causes have you let go of?

- What are your favorite project memories—tasks, mile-stones, initiatives—that have come about from your charitable giving and volunteering?

- Do you feel that you are fulfilling your purpose for being alive with this generous work?

Hopefully, you'll see progress in your experience of connection and gratification. If not, return to your Generosity Gameplan and see where it may be out of alignment with your headline issues, your relationships, and your strengths.

## Exercise 16: Evaluate the Impact of Your Gifts

There's a delicate balance to evaluating the impact of your gifts. On the one hand, as Frank Hanna says, it may not be possible to measure the effects of transcendent work. "If you're going to be generous, you need to have a certain amount of tolerance for not seeing the results, because they happen in the spiritual and not the physical realm. But when you're investing in the human soul, that pays dividends forever. That's the benefit."

Having faith in results you can't see requires humility. Kent Bergemann is very conscious of the power differential that exists when giving significant financial resources to an organization. He doesn't want to use evaluation as a stick or a vehicle for ego. "Pride is a very subtle thing," he says. "Having financial resources is a tremendous responsibility and burden. But using the fact that I have the money and you want it can be dangerous."

On the other hand, we do need to practice good steward-ship and scrutiny where we can. "I'm not going to throw money down a hole and have someone abuse that gift," Kent says. There are some simple checks you can make to ensure that your giving is effective:

- Look for benefits to people served and not just the features of the programs delivered. Ask the people served whether their lives have been changed.

- Look for leadership, especially on the governing board, that is making strategic decisions, not management decisions. Governing boards have the responsibility to set strategy, provide direction, and access capital for a nonprofit. Often times, boards get too close to the action and meddle in the management. This is a caution sign that the management is not doing its job or that the board does not understand its role.

> Look for benefits to people served and not just the features of the programs delivered.

- Expect behavior from senior leadership that is responsive to donors.

## Reflect on Your Results: Examples

My friend Les Weil has been heavily involved in community development and fundraising in Milwaukee. He knows the world of nonprofits from the inside, so he's especially sensitive to the results of his own gifts. "I make major gifts once a year, and one of the things I look for is a thank-you note. If I don't get one, I stop giving. My wife thinks I'm being petty, but to me it's a sign of the kind of organization it is. I don't just want to hear from them once a year when they're asking for another gift. I want to have a relationship with them. People don't give their best gift the first time—they're waiting to see, 'Am I appreciated? Is my gift handled properly?'"

Another thing that Les looks for is volunteer participation. He says, "If I meet with an executive director and there's no volunteer there, that's one demerit point. There should be a real partnership between the board, the staff, and the volunteers. Board members aren't just there to show up at the meeting, have lunch, and leave implementation to the staff. And if I find that a staff person isn't following up, I don't want to waste my time. It's partly our fault as a social sector. We haven't laid out the roles and responsibilities properly." Les is convinced that strong connections are a marker of success in nonprofit organizations, and he's not afraid to prioritize them.

When I asked Dave Romoser about gratification, he shared this story. Dave has served on the board of an inner-city early childhood education center for nine years, two of those as board chair. "We needed to change up leadership at the top, and we did," he says. "I led the board in doing what we all knew we needed to do." The new executive director has been with the center for three years now. At a recent meeting, this director, a staff person, and a board member were reporting to the past directors on the state of the organization and the initiatives that were going on. "We were all so pleased with what the organization has achieved and the direction it's going," says Dave. "Driving back from that meeting, I said to myself, 'That is the most important payback.' To see the outcome of your thousands of hours of volunteering and thousands of dollars in donations. Outcomes, outcomes, outcomes, that's what drives me. People have told me that my skill set is as a change agent, and I'm flattered by that." Dave knows which results he cares about, and that adds a lot to his sense of purpose in giving.

Sometimes you need to step things up and get a formal, professional evaluation of a program. Calvin Edwards had a donor client who became concerned about a nonprofit after he joined the board. His family had donated some $15 million to this organization, which then developed a program in India tailored to their giving priorities. To follow up on his concerns, the donor engaged Calvin's firm to scrutinize the program and report findings. They went to India and spent 33 person-days interviewing staff, clients, and beneficiaries. "The situation was complex: there was lots of good being done, but there were also problems and unanswered questions," Calvin says. "We spelled out the good and the bad to the donor, and also provided a remediation plan that recommended that he not continue to support the program unless the organization took certain remedial actions."

Calvin was expecting the donor to say, "Great, let's do this 10-point remediation plan." Instead, his response was, "I have many people who want my money, and I don't need to give it to people who need remediation plans. I'm going somewhere else." This response was a surprise to Calvin, but he could understand it. "There's value in due diligence," he says. "You get information that helps you decide what you want to do. I'd think, 'I've invested my $15 million, and I want to make good on that rather than back out.' This donor had a different mind-set, temperament, and net worth, and his decision was to move on." To me, this story demonstrates the importance of knowing and being true to your own Generosity Gameplan. That's the only way to find the connection and meaning that will sustain you.

# Study in Generosity:
# Phoebe Cade Miles and Richard Miles

Phoebe Cade Miles and Richard Miles' story exemplifies strategic generosity. I met this husband-and-wife team over breakfast at The Philanthropy Roundtable, a national association for donors and foundation trustees, where we bonded over a conversation about the importance of strong families and healthy marriages. Phoebe and Richard dedicate their days to stewarding the abundance they've been blessed with through the Gloria Dei Foundation and their latest project, the Cade Museum of Creativity + Invention.

## Exploring Their Heart and History

Phoebe doesn't have to look far to find the inspiration and means for the generous life she shares with Richard. Her father, the late Dr. Robert Cade, was a physician, philanthropist, and the lead inventor of Gatorade, the sports beverage. The proceeds of that innovation form the family's financial inheritance, and Dr. Cade's example of exceptional giving is their spiritual inheritance.

"My parents were generous to a fault, which I didn't even know was possible," says Phoebe. "My dad believed that his role was to help anyone with a need who came across his path, to the point where we sometimes didn't have money in the bank. He didn't ask questions or worry about details, and what I saw as a child was just the tip of the iceberg."

In her hometown of Gainesville, Florida, people still approach Phoebe with stories of her father's acts of kindness. She says, "One of Dad's kidney patients lived an hour and a half away and couldn't come for dialysis and other regular treatments because he had to take public transit, which was difficult for him. So my dad bought him a car!" Another time, Dr. Cade bought an entire set of musical instruments for a public school that wanted to start an orchestra. That ready and unquestioning approach to giving was inspired by the parable of the Good Samaritan, which resonated very strongly with Dr. Cade.

Phoebe also learned the importance of collaboration from her father's business experiences. Dr. Cade had thousands of ideas for new inventions, but Gatorade was the most successful because he had the right team around him. "They knew how to place the product in the market, how to negotiate a contract, and how to get a trademark," she says. "It doesn't matter how great your idea is—it won't work unless you have the right people supporting you."

## Developing Their Gameplan

Later in life, Dr. Cade's giving became more structured, and he eventually hired a financial planner to put him on a philanthropic budget. Seeing this progression helped Phoebe and her siblings realize that it was better to exercise wisdom in choosing whom to help. Prior to Dr. Cade's passing in 2007, his children recognized that their father's legacy of giving risked being diluted if his financial resources were parceled out six ways. The Cade siblings wanted to find a way to give as a group and maximize their impact, so they set up the Gloria Dei Foundation in 2004 to serve as the vehicle for their charity.

With Gloria Dei, the Cade siblings were determined to uphold the philosophy behind their parents' generosity. The foundation holds true to a Christian mission while the second generation of Cades looks for ways to refine the giving process, honing the administrative and organizational aspects of their philanthropy.

Not wanting to turn anyone away, they found that their initial gifts were scattershot, and thus the impacts were harder to measure. Through a combination of trial and error and consultation with more established family foundations, the Cade siblings learned that giving larger amounts to fewer organizations led to greater potential for transformation. For example, at one point they were contributing to 12 different Lutheran colleges scattered around the country. "It was hard to see the effects of the gifts because they were relatively small," Phoebe says. "Of course, the colleges still wanted the donations, but we decided to tie things together and concentrate on one area."

One result was a large lead gift to the Fisher House Foundation, which builds guest housing close to veteran's hospitals. Fisher House shoulders the cost of construction, and afterward the veteran's hospital picks up the operational cost. "That large lead gift enabled the community to go out and get close to a matching amount from the rest of the community," Richard says. "A great partnership all around."

The Cade family is also developing a museum for creativity and invention. Although this is not specifically a Christian organization, they feel they are honoring Christian principles through this work. "We feel that if you're blessed, you should be a blessing, and that goes in the scientific world as well," Phoebe says. "We want to inspire creative thinking, future inventors, and early entrepreneurs."

> "We want to inspire creative thinking, future inventors, and early entrepreneurs."

To publicize and start executing on the museum's mission even before they have a building, the Cade family established a $50,000 annual innovation prize for start-ups that targets early researchers and entrepreneurs. "We're focused on getting ideas out of the lab and into the marketplace," says Richard. "Last year we had 120 applications from around the state—these folks have a good idea and some demonstration that the idea works, and we want to give them incentive to get a company going or take their idea to the next level."

The prize also supports the educational mission of the museum. "We want to get the participants, researchers and inventors, into middle school and high school classrooms to teach students about the science behind their inventions and the potential impact," says Richard. "That way, learning is more fun, and kids see the importance between having an idea and actually spreading it and commercializing it."

Creating clear visions for Gloria Dei and the Cade Museum of Creativity + Invention has also helped Phoebe, Richard, and the other Cade siblings clarify their individual giving. They've committed to tithing from their own resources to causes that are important to them. One sister is very interested in animal welfare and preventing abuse, and since that work doesn't fit with Gloria Dei's mission, she supports it through her personal donations. Another brother is keen on veterans' affairs, so he contributes to that.

## Reflecting on Their Results

Richard and Phoebe find great fulfillment in their shared philanthropic work. In 2009, Richard took a year-long sabbatical from the Foreign Service that became a full-time commitment to the Cade Museum and other family efforts. "This work has been a lot more interesting and exciting than what I was doing before," he says.

The couple moved their family home from Washington, DC back to Gainesville so they could be physically present where the work and relationships were happening. "When we put our gifts together, we're able to get a lot done," says Phoebe. "I relate very well to people and get excited about a vision, and Richard has the administrative capabilities to carry that vision out methodically." Spending their strengths together on their headline issues of health, creativity, and education has been a consuming and satisfying endeavor for them.

To evaluate results, Gloria Dei has put practices in place to hold organizations accountable, including site visits and assessments of activities and events. They follow up with questions about how grant money was spent and how effectiveness is measured. Many foundations value family harmony above impact, Richard says, and try to keep everyone happy at the expense of creating change. The Cade family has educated themselves by attending philanthropic conferences and reading books so they can incorporate best practices in the way they run the foundation and museum.

Focusing on connected generosity has led to clarity and success as well. "Being involved helps us evaluate the impact and make better decisions about where to give," says Phoebe. "Meeting the founders and seeing where they're going is bar none the best way to determine the direction and leadership of an organization. I understand now why business people travel so much, because when you're doing a deal, you have to see the person across the table."

> "Meeting the founders and seeing where they're going is bar none the best way to determine the direction and leadership of an organization."

The Cade family is looking ahead to the giving legacy they will pass on to the third generation. Phoebe and Richard's daughter Cecelia has been hired by Gloria Dei to help create a junior board for the grandchildren between the ages of 16 and 30 so they can take part and begin learning about intentional giving and finding consensus. And if some of the grandchildren aren't in alignment with the Christian mission of Gloria Dei, they will be invited to work with the museum or the community foundation.

Phoebe and Richard, together with the rest of their family, have discovered the joys of crafting and executing a Generosity Gameplan that truly reflects their passions and strengths. Their openness to learning and pursuing excellence in giving has helped them capably steward the generous legacy that Dr. Cade and his wife passed on to them.

# Jim and Lauren's Generosity Gameplan

Working through the steps of the Generosity Gameplan process, Jim and Lauren created this generosity mission together:

> *We feel strongly about helping causes related to urban economic development and health and wellness. Our generosity specifically addresses the needs of the entrepreneurial poor who need coaching and the elderly who need care. We envision fulfilling our generous goals with small and established nonprofit organizations and churches in our city that are committed to vibrant self-sufficient neighborhoods and elders who are honored and cared for.*

In the early stages of developing their Generosity Gameplan, Jim and Lauren got clear on their strengths. Jim always thought of himself as a leader, which is correct, but seeing himself through his spiritual gifts, it was clear that teaching was a strength too. "Enabling others to reach their potential" was music to his ears and a confidence-builder for him as he worked with men and women who wanted to start small businesses in the city—he was their teacher.

Lauren, on the other hand, was able to take her natural ability as an encourager and bring it to the elderly she cared for and the organization leaders she worked with. She finds great satisfaction in nurturing others with her presence.

Jim and Lauren were amazed when they took an inventory of their currencies. Before, they were always asking, "How much time can we give up?" and "How much money can we afford to spread around?" Now, their abundance of relationships is front-and-center too. At first, the sheer number of people they knew was a little overwhelming, but soon after choosing only a few friends to start with, the bridges they built were fruitful. One in particular was a friend who had loved the ballet for years as a patron but wanted to become more involved. Jim and Lauren built a bridge with one of their daughter's dance instructors who was also a director at the ballet. Imagine their surprise when these two new connections discovered that they also shared an interest in clean water for northern Uganda, of all things.

Headlines were always in front of Jim and Lauren, but always from the same news sources, right of center. When they intentionally added center-left sources for the same headline, they got a fresh perspective on an issue and were able to make decisions that were better informed and less one-sided. Jim had always relied on his favorite inner city alderman for insights on who needed help. When he added the local sheriff to the conversation, he got another view of the population's needs and what the barriers might be for them.

Jim had served on an inner city private school board for many years. The 80 Hispanic boys in the school were from immigrant families making their start in this country who longed for their children to be well educated. The school made a commitment to every rising fifth grade boy to help them get up to speed in two languages, reading, science, and math and to prepare them to graduate from a local Catholic high school.

Jim had been part of saving boys' lives one at a time for nearly 15 years. Now, with his clear and focused Generosity Gameplan, he offered himself to the parent-teacher association (PTA) instead of directly to the boys. He resigned from the board and served the PTA members as a mentor and coach when an individual parent wanted to start a business.

After some time of living into their Generosity Gameplan, Jim and Lauren took time to reflect on their effectiveness. They made a few adjustments in who they helped and increased the relationship bridges they made. Then, one night at dinner, they remembered that they wanted to equip their daughters to accelerate their already generous lives now as well as leaving them contributions through their estate. Partnering with the local community foundation, they found a willing advisor to help them establish three donor-advised funds. Now their daughters can add to them over time and live out their own Generosity Gameplans.

# Conclusion

*"Ever since knowing that a group of very different people loving one another was potentially repeatable, I have never been able to feel totally hopeless about the human condition."* M. Scott Peck, *The Different Drum*

Jesus sending his disciples out two by two, employees forming teams to accomplish goals, neighbors working together to clean up after a crisis, a church community supporting a family in need, homeless connecting at the recuse mission—in generosity as in all aspects of life, context matters. Generosity rightly understood is done with others, not for others. Relationships change our generosity.

My hope is that this view of generosity can awaken a longing and be an antidote for autonomy from others and God. My hope is that you can move from seeing generosity as a check-writing and volunteering adventure to living and being generous in ways that expand your life and the lives of others. My hope is that the three currencies of relationships, strengths, and resources can be mobilized for a generous future.

> Generosity rightly understood is done with others, not for others.

When you honor your heart's desire for connection, spend your renewable currencies of relationships, strengths, and resources, and invest in ways that make use of the multiplier effect, you are practicing connected generosity. Connected generosity transforms you and the world in three ways: through richer relationships, gratifying acts of service, and effective giving.

## Richer Relationships

When connection is the starting point for generosity, your relationships will naturally become stronger, deeper, and more satisfying. Psychologists Debra Oswald and Eddie Clark have found in their research that there are four necessary behaviors for strengthening relationships, and each of these behaviors is built into connected generosity.

- **Openness** comes in the form of exploring your heart and history and sharing that with others. When you tell people your personal connection to a cause, you are bringing them close to what matters to you. This often prompts a similar self-disclosure on their part. And when you give from your passions, others can see and respond to the real you, rather than a cool, detached persona that you might maintain when giving for other reasons.

- **Supportiveness** comes in the action you take to create change on a mutual cause. You'll see each other's efforts as supporting your collective desire to meet needs and relieve suffering. And you will also become more aware of people's personal needs that you can help them with.

- **Interaction** is part of working together on a common project. The more involved you are, the more opportunities you have to talk, email, share meals, and develop affection for your colleagues at an organization and the people you serve.

- **Positivity** is inherent in the hopeful posture we take in our giving. Operating from a common belief that change is possible, looking for solutions rather than complaining, and encouraging each other in our endeavors—all of these contribute to positivity.

The focus you bring to your Generosity Gameplan will also help you concentrate on your most rewarding relationships. When you are more present with people, those bonds will be that much more valuable.

## Gratifying Acts of Service

Connected generosity feels more meaningful because of the richer relationships it fosters, and also because it taps into our unique sense of purpose and calling. We get a sense of gratification from charitable giving and volunteering that has these characteristics:

- **We're using our strengths.** Playing at the top of our game and getting intrinsic pleasure from the philanthropic work we do is deeply rewarding.

- **The work feels important.** Making a difference—positively affecting one person's experience—carries a certain amount of satisfaction. But creating real change  improving an organization, a neighborhood, a population, a system—feels even more worthwhile.

- **We are uniquely needed for the task.** The closer the fit between our history, personality, and skills and the philanthropic work we take on, the more valued and useful we feel.

- **We see how our efforts fit into the larger scheme of things.** When we know the role that each donation and event plays within our Generosity Gameplan, together they take on more significance. And when we understand how our own philanthropy combines with that of others to effect change, that can be tremendously motivating.

Intentionally living out our purpose through our generosity is a recipe for thriving.

## Effective Giving

We want our generosity to do as much good as possible, and making connection the core of our giving strategy helps us with that goal in a number of ways:

- **Focus:** Creating a Generosity Gameplan that zeroes in on our heart's desire makes it clearer why we say no to causes that are not a priority for us. And it's easier to stay current and evaluate outcomes when we're dealing with fewer projects and organizations.

- **Insight:** When we connect with program and board leaders, we get a deeper understanding about what works and why. Connections with those being served give us real-time knowledge about how lives are being changed.

- **Patience:** Familiarity with organizational priorities gives us patience when the inevitable speed bumps happen along the way.

- **Passion:** When we care more about our giving targets, we put more attention and energy into making sure those targets are met.

Since we rarely see the long-term effects of our generosity, evaluating near-term results becomes more important, and possible, when we're intimately connected to the people, projects, and causes we support.

I'll close with a gospel story from St. Luke that captures the movement of a generous spirit from caution to connection to abundance.

On the shore of Lake Gennesaret, the crowds pressed Jesus for more. More insights, more healing, more miracles. So Jesus asked Peter to put his boat a short distance away from shore so he could teach from there.

After teaching for some time, Jesus asked Peter to *duc in altum*—"Put out into the deep"—so they could fish. Peter resisted because he had just returned from an unsuccessful fishing venture, but he obeyed.

The subsequent catch was so amazing that another boat had to help because the nets were tearing.

> After teaching for some time, Jesus asked Peter to *duc in altum*—"Put out into the deep."

Peter, now in touch with his heart's desire, made himself available to Jesus, and Jesus responded with a generous invitation: "Put out into the deep with me, and I'll make you a catcher of men and women instead of fish."

This is a compelling story of listening to our heart's desire, making ourselves available, and acting. *Duc in altum!* Let us launch our generosity into deep water and prepare to be amazed at what comes forth.

# Acknowledgments

Called, moved, inspired, urged—all of these words describe the impetus for getting this content from my heart and head into some form that could be shared. The journey has been exhilarating and humbling. Why? Because those closest to me demonstrated what St. Ignatius called magis, meaning "more"—not doing more but being more for others, being generous to me with their insights and affirmations, compliments and criticisms. In fact, much of this work could be rightly called crowdsourced. When I called on friends to respond to my ideas, 75 of them did so. As iron sharpens iron, so did the crowd of friends listed here make this content rich and validated.

Others invested abundant time by being interviewed, adding proof that pushing the refresh button on generosity is timely and important: Tom Beerntsen, Kent and Linda Bergemann, Julia Bolz, Calvin Edwards, John and Barb Findley, Frank Hanna, Gordon Hartmann, Harville Hendrix and Helen LaKelly Hunt, John and Sherri Kasdorf, Mike Klonne, Richard and Phoebe Miles, Dave Romoser, Paul Schervish, and Les Weil.

Long days spent in New York, Chicago, Dallas, Abiquiú, New Mexico, and Boston with my mentors and advisors, Adrian Duffy at Strategic Coach, Dr. Paul Schervish, Monsignor Don Fischer, Dr. Claire Gaudiani, Dr. Harville Hendrix and Helen LaKelly Hunt—all of these friends inspired me and gave me clarity and confidence.

After 25 years of marriage, Jamee, my wife, told me one day that it had just dawned on her that not every idea I have is a good one. Thankfully, she and the rest of my family—my children, Karen and Micah, my sister, Anne, and my mom, Josie—were always encouraging about this one.

As an entrepreneur, my skill-set is to cast a vision, chart a course, and get projects to 80%, but I need able pros to help me finish. What a team I had! Long-term colleagues Jessica Gorecki and Pat Woehrer contributed and ran interference for me while this work was getting done. We have been connected for much good. Brenda Leifso has added confidence to our work with her editing, and Mike Luedke helped me get things out of my head and actually on paper in the beginning.

My personal business coach, Susan Englehutt, effectively guided, directed, and connected me to people and strategy to launch the effort to inspire the Generosity Gameplan®. Susan could see that, if the book was ever to get from concept to reality, I would need someone with whom I shared values and aspirations, and that turned out to be her fellow Canadian Alison Gresik. When we started writing together, Alison was somewhere in central Europe with her husband and two children on what she called an *extended journey,* after selling home and possessions a year earlier. By the time we finished the manuscript, her journey was on hiatus and she now lives in Vancouver, BC. Susan was good to us both in making the connection for our benefit, not hers.

So there you have it: a crowd, mentors, family, advisors, helpers, friends have all made this possible. Many thanks and God's blessings to you.

The crowd: Rafeal Andrews, Luke Austenfeld, Ted Baehr, Scott Beck, Tom Beerntsen, Kent Bergemann, Konnie Boulter, Anne Bristol, Scott Bristol, Steve Brock, Jack Christ, Dan Cobb, Tom Curl, Anne Derber, Kay Edwards, Barbara Elliott, Bill Eyster, Jared Faellaci, David Ferguson, Jeff Fray, Deborah Fugenschuh, Alan Gaudynski, Paula Hare, Rick Harig, Jon Helminiak, Harville Hendrix, Mike Hogan, Gregg Hunter, Ron Jones, Richard Kane, Sam Kennedy, David Krill, David Larson, Tom Livergood, Linda Maris, Mary Kay Mark, Margaret McCarthy, James Mc-

Cormack, Sarah Miller, Brian Mosley, Scott Murray, Ned Nagy, Dawn Nuoffer, Jim Otepka, Jennifer Pope, Dave Romoser, Gary Rosberg, Carol Roth, George Roth, Paul Schervish, Kevin Siefert, Brother Bob Smith, Jamee Stanley, Karen Stanley, Scott Stanley, Charles Stetson, Maureen Sullivan, Rose Sweet, Stan Swim, Josie Toogood, Shannon Toronto, Rajan Trafton, Steve Trafton, Teddie Ussery, Jeff Van Beaver, Bruce Ward, Sheila Weber, Jude Werra, W. Bradford Wilcox, Pat Woehrer, John Zentgraf.

# Endnotes

1. The inspiration for the starfish story comes from the writings of Loren Eiseley, although if you read the original, you'll find it has a much different message!

2. The term *men and women for others* was introduced on July 31, 1973, the feast day of St. Ignatius, by Jesuit Superior General Father Pedro Arrupe, who was speaking to the Tenth International Congress of Jesuit Alumni of Europe. The concept is now foundational for Jesuit education worldwide, and schools strive to ensure that each student graduates with a strong sense of social justice.

3. You can find out more about Jim Collins' ideas for improving social efforts in his monograph *Good to Great and the Social Sectors.*

4. I have Steve Brock to thank for this insight on the Millennial Generation's devotion to volunteering.

5. From "Philanthropy's 3 Percent Solution," *Philanthropy Magazine,* Fall 2012.

6. I'd like to thank my friend Mary Kay Mark from Northern Trust for her insights on nonprofit financials.

7. The tip about gauging your importance as a donor by whom you meet with comes from my friend Jon Helminiak.

8. From the webinar "The Artful Solicitor: Successful Major Gifts Moves Management" by David A. Mersky (nonprofitwebinars.com).

9. National Center for Charitable Statistics, researched by Marquette University Social Innovation Initiative, 2013.

10. For more on starting generosity early, I highly recommend the book *Generous Kids: Helping Your Child Experience the Joy of Giving* by Colleen O'Donnell and Lyn Baker.

11. "The World's Billionaires," *Forbes Magazine,* 2012.

12. Thanks to Mike Hogan for reminding me of this link between wealth and identity.

13. The website for Rick Harig's organization, Legacy Resources, is legacy-resources.com.

14. Thanks to Shannon Toronto for sharing this C.S. Lewis quotation with me.

15. This prayer is sometimes attributed to Óscar Romero, but it was actually written by Bishop Untener for a homily given by Cardinal John Dearden in November 1979 for a celebration of departed priests.

16. "The Brain on Love," March 24, 2012, Opinionator, *The New York Times* (opinionator.blogs.nytimes.com/2012/03/24/the-brain-on-love/).

17. The Science of Generosity initiative at the University of Notre Dame funds studies of generosity such as Bradford Wilcox's. You can find them at GenerosityResearch.nd.edu.

18. You can learn more about Rose Sweet's work on restoring broken relationships at RoseSweet.com.

19. From "Creating a Moral Biography of Wealth: A Conversation with Paul G. Schervish" in *The Whitepapers: Quarterly Intelligence for Informed Investors,* Spring 2005.

20. "The Dunbar Number, from the Guru of Social Networks" by Drake Bennett for Businessweek.com.

21. *The Catholic Spiritual Gifts Inventory,* Sherry Weddell, The Sienna Institute Press.

# More Resources

Here are some of my favorite resources on charitable giving and volunteering to help you develop and live out your Generosity Gameplan.

## Books

*Generous Kids: Helping Your Child Experience the Joy of Giving,* by Colleen O'Donnell and Lyn Baker. A fun read of practical tips and insights, organized by age. http://www.generouskids.com

*The Greater Good: How Philanthropy Drives the American Economy and Can Save Capitalism,* by Claire Gaudiani. http://www.clairegaudiani.com

## Organizations

**Generous Church,** an organization launched by the National Christian Foundation, offers resources for church leaders to lead conversations about generosity. http://www.generouschurch.com

**National Center for Family Philanthropy** in Washington, D.C. provides research, expertise, and learning opportunities to families who give and those that work with them. http://www.ncfp.org

**Grantmakers for Effective Organizations** in Washington, D.C. promotes strategies and practices that contribute to grantee success. http://www.geofunders.org

**Forum of Regional Association of Grantmakers** in Arlington, VA is a network of 34 regional associations of grantmakers that leverages members' collective resources. Contact info@givingforum.org. http://www.givingforum.org

**Association of Small Foundations** in Washington, D.C. is a membership organization for donors, trustees, employees, and consultants of foundations that have few or no staff. http://www.smallfoundations.org

**Philanthropy Roundtable** in Washington, D.C. strengthens the free society through the promotion of excellence in philanthropy. http://www.philanthropyroundtable.org

**Council on Foundations in Arlington,** VA strives to increase the effectiveness of the nonprofit sector by providing support to foundations, corporations, and philanthropic entities. http://www.cof.org

## Initiatives and Conferences

**Why Not Me** empowers circles of friends and communities of all types to give together and count their change. http://www.whynotme.me

**Generous Giving.** Through retreats and regional and national conferences, Generous Giving spreads the Biblical message of generosity among those entrusted with much. http://www.generousgiving.org

**The Gathering** offers an annual conference to expand the vision and effectiveness in giving among Christian givers. http://www.thegathering.com